TEXAS
OFF-ROAD RACING

A FATHER-SON JOURNEY TO A SIDE-BY-SIDE CHAMPIONSHIP

M I K E   K O W I S ,   E s q .

TEXAS OFF-ROAD RACING:
A Father-Son Journey to
a Side-by-Side Championship
Copyright © 2020 Mike Kowis, Esq.

Library of Congress Control Number: 2020906198
ISBN-13: 978-1-7328630-2-6 (paperback
ISBN-13: 978-1-7328630-3-3 (eBook/MOBI format)

www.mikekowis.com

Lecture PRO Publishing
Conroe, Texas

Dedication

This book is
dedicated to amateur
off-road racers who put their blood,
sweat, *and wallets* on the line
in every competition. God
speed to us all!

Testimonials

Here's what people are saying about Texas Off-road Racing:

"This book reminds me of The Fast and the Furious, but without the fast." – Mike's literary agent

"Texas Off-road Racing is the best book I've ever read!" –Mike's mom

"OMG! You took our son off-road racing??? I thought you guys went fishing." –Mike's shocked wife

"Mike always loved a good book with pictures." –Mike's kindergarten teacher

"This book does for off-road racing what the Segway did for mass transportation." – a disappointed racing fan

"I used to think Mike couldn't write well, and this book confirms it." –Mike's 12th grade English teacher

"What does Mike know about racing? He thought the Baja 1000 was the name of his favorite salad dressing." – Mike's high school principal

"I'm not saying that Mike lacks passion, but he put the dead in Dead Poet's Society." – Mike's yoga instructor

"Daaaaang! Mike Kowis is one fast dude." –said no one ever

But seriously, you're gonna love this book. Go ahead and read it now… I double-dog dare you!

Contents

INTRODUCTION

The first time *I fell in love* was the day that I brought home "Big Red" – a brand-spanking-new, red 1984 Honda 200s three-wheeler. As a young boy growing up in the country, all I ever wanted was an all-terrain vehicle ("ATV") to call my own. So, I did yard work on the weekends until I finally saved enough money for my dream machine. All those Saturdays that I sacrificed to pay for it made me appreciate Big Red even more.

From the first day, Big Red and I were inseparable. Together with my friends who owned ATVs (including close friend and neighbor Chuck Willingham), we explored the thick piney woods and endless sandbars along the Trinity River near my home in Kenefick, Texas. Like Huckleberry Finn and Tom Sawyer, we were searching for freedom and adventure. These were truly the glory days of my early teenage years, and I relished every minute of it.

With Big Red as my trusty steed, I occasionally competed in ATV rodeos held at a nearby horse arena in Liberty, Texas. These events offered a variety of timed challenges for ATV riders, such as obstacle courses and barrel races. Believe it or not, I still have the trophies from those amateur competitions and proudly display them in my garage. They represent good times and bring back fond memories from my adventurous youth.

My spoils from competing in ATV rodeos as a young lad. Good times!

After getting a driver's license at the ripe old age of 15 and a half, I reluctantly sold Big Red and used the money to purchase my first car, a 1977 Ford Granada four-door sedan. I swapped riding the wooded trails for running the public roads with my high school friends... well, at least the ones like Chuck who didn't mind being seen in an old, rusty Ford Granada.

In 2001, I got the off-road bug again and bought a new Honda TRX 250ex four-wheeler to explore the wooded trails behind my neighborhood. Once again, this red ATV reminded me of all the fun that I previously had with Big Red. What a great way to relive my youth!

A few years later, I discovered an off-road competition for ATVs and dirt bikes called cross-country ("XC") racing. For those unfamiliar, (local) XC racing is typically a one-hour race set on a three to five mile course over natural terrain. Off-road racers battle through tight woods, open pastures, muddy creek crossings, rocky hills, and other challenging obstacles. The object is to complete the most laps in the least amount of time.

Win or lose, it is an accomplishment just to finish one of these rugged XC races. In fact, it is common to see at least a handful of racers throw in the towel early due to mechanical failures, tire problems, collisions with trees or other racers, or after becoming hopelessly stuck in a nasty mud hole.

In 2004, I competed in my first cross-country ATV race at Round 1 of the Grand National Cross Country ("GNCC") series held in Gilmer, Texas (see www.gnccracing.com for more info). At the time, I had no idea that a GNCC race was a big deal and that it regularly drew hundreds of spectators, media, and competitors from all over the country. In fact, some of the GNCC competitors had factory sponsorships and a full race team to support them on the course. As for little ol' me, my race team consisted of just one person — my childhood buddy and one heck of an ATV racer himself, Mike Vyoral. At this race, Mike played double duty as both my mechanic and moral supporter (to make sure I didn't chicken out when the GNCC announcer yelled, "10 seconds!").

Photo Credit: Racedaypix / Climbing a steep hill during my first GNCC race.

Before the big race started, I was feeling nervous about my first appearance in a XC race. Because this was a national level event, I would be racing that day against some of the top competitors in the country. Those big names drew huge crowds of spectators that spread out along the rugged 11-mile course. They were everywhere! Many fans hung out near the starting line, while others lined up along the course near steep hill climbs, muddy creek crossings, or other treacherous spots. Seeing these top ATV racers and the large crowds made my first attempt at XC racing even more nerve-wracking.

At this race, I quickly discovered that GNCC fans are a little different. They don't simply watch the action from the sidelines and take pics. Whenever duty calls, they jump onto the course to help racers who get stuck in the mud or need an extra push to reach the top of a hill climb. These folks are more than just mere spectators; they are true fanatics and become part of the event.

While waiting in line for tech inspection (where GNCC race officials inspect my ATV for the required safety equipment), I noticed the person behind me was a well-known GNCC racer, Scott Kilby. I couldn't believe it! I had followed reports of the top GNCC racers for over a year, and Scott was one of the top riders in the Utility Modified class at that time. Somehow, I got the courage to introduce myself and asked him for a few words of wisdom as I take on my first XC race. Scott smiled and said that my goal should not be to win. Rather, I should just try my best to finish the race and have fun in the process. Turns out, that was great advice and it took some of the pressure off.

While I didn't reach the podium that day, I did finish the two-hour race and loved every heart-pounding moment. More important, I was immediately hooked on the sport and have since competed in 13 seasons of cross-country racing on either ATVs or Utility Terrain Vehicles ("UTVs"). The one piece of advice that Scott failed to mention was that this sport is as addictive as it is fun!

A year later, I returned to the GNCC when they came back to Gilmer, Texas for their 2005 season opener. At this event, I met several more famous off-road racers, such as legendary ATV racer, Mike Penland. At that time, Mike was already well-known for his many GNCC championships and other off-road racing titles, and he was frequently interviewed for off-road magazines.

Photo Credit: Racedaypix / Launching off a small hill during my second GNCC race.

The next day, I was lucky enough to get my picture taken with Mike when I competed against him, Scott Kilby, and many others at The 2005 Maxxis 6 Hours of Texas ATV race (which had a unique Le Mans-style start!) in Greenville, Texas. What an honor it was to meet and race against an off-road racing legend and my ATV racing hero!

Mike Penland & Me @ The Maxxis 6 Hours of Texas (Scott Kilby in the background).

Turns out that Mike is as nice of a guy off the track as he is a fierce competitor on the track. I later called him from time to time to ask questions about wrenching on my ATV, and he always stopped whatever he was doing to answer my questions. He is a gentleman and truly represents what this sport is all about.

From 2004 until 2008, I competed in the Utility ATV class of the (now defunct) All-Terrain Vehicle Cross-Country Series ("ATVCCS") ran by David and Gayle Culpepper. This series hosted ATV races in East Texas that were ridiculously fun.

It's a bird. It's a plane. It's me jumping my Kawasaki Prairie during an ATVCCS race.

The ATVCCS was a godsend for off-roader racers like me. Without this local ATV series, my choices were to travel thousands of miles to compete in GNCC races that were primarily located along the East Coast of the United States, or not race at all. There might have been local ATV series in other states, but at that time I was unaware of them (remember, this was before the Internet was popular).

I quickly discovered that racers in the ATVCCS series were super supportive and friendly (as is true with all of the XC series that I've competed in thus far). The only thing I didn't enjoy about this series was the eight-hour round trip that it took for me to reach each race from my house. This made for a very long day on race days (usually Sundays). After five seasons with the ATVCCS, I reluctantly hung up my helmet due to burnout from all the travel.

Splashing through the mud in my early days of XC racing with the ATVCCS. Fun stuff!

After a three-year break, I picked up my helmet again and began ATV racing in 2012 with the Texas Off-Road National ("TORN") series (see www.tornracing.com for more info). Similar to the ATVCCS, the TORN series is loads of fun and operated by great people (the Kirchmeier family). This series hosts races in the greater Dallas-Ft. Worth area, which often meant a 10-hour round trip for me. Ugh. Despite the long drives, I was thrilled to be racing once again and hanging out with fellow off-road enthusiasts.

Photo Credit: PDMokry / This motley crew of TORN racers includes me on my green Kawasaki KFX.

The TORN races were going smoothly until the summer of 2014 when I had a devastating accident that rocked my world. During a race near the Texas-Oklahoma border, I made an aggressive pass of not one, but two ATVs in an open pasture. To get around both, I stayed on the throttle a bit too long. After passing the second racer at 40-plus miles per hour, I looked up and saw a four-strand, barbed-wire fence just ahead of me. My heart sank as I immediately realized my mistake. There was simply not enough time to slow down and make the sharp left turn before reaching the fence. There was absolutely no doubt in my mind that this barbed-wire fence would be the end of me. Gulp!

The next few seconds are still a blur in my mind, but I recall slamming on my brakes and turning the handlebars as quickly as possible. Suddenly, my 600 lb. race quad began rolling violently towards the fence straight ahead, and I was thrown hard onto the ground in front of the ATV. Everything gets fuzzy at this point, but I still remember tumbling towards the fence and praying that I would somehow survive.

When I came to a stop, I was lying on the ground 10 feet on the other side of the fence. I looked up and saw aluminum skid plates and four tires (the underside of my ATV) leaning against the fence. The top two strands of barbed wire were bunched together up high, and the same thing happened to the bottom two strands down low. I looked down at my torso and found three sets of holes in my padded chest protector where the barbed wire penetrated the fabric. To my utter amazement, my body somehow rolled through the middle of the barbed-wire fence, and I miraculously walked away with only a broken right wrist, plus a few scrapes and bruises. The only logical explanation I have for surviving this horrific crash was that the big guy upstairs was watching out for me that day. Thank you, Jesus!

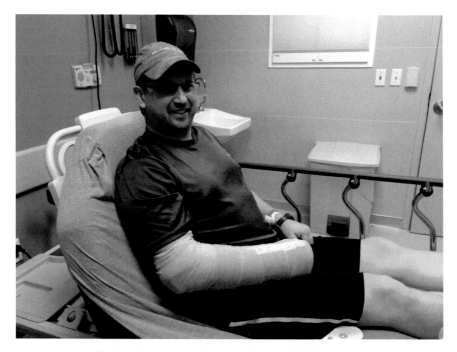

According to the x-rays, my last ATV race resulted in a broken wrist and a shattered ego. Ouchie!

The two racers I just passed in the field immediately stopped to check on me and render aid, if needed. Until that day, I had never met these guys and didn't expect them to put their race on hold for me. But they did anyway, and I really appreciated their kindness. I told them I would be fine and to keep racing. This is the kind of sportsmanship that I find to be commonplace in off-road racing. Most everyone I meet is there to have a good time and win races, but they are more concerned about their fellow racers' safety and well-being.

Afterwards, I wasn't sure if my wife would ever let me race again. She said I could keep my quad for trail riding, but preferred that my ATV racing days were over for good. I didn't want to hear that, but completely understood where she was coming from. Thanks to this accident, I finally realized that this hobby I so dearly loved could potentially jeopardize my health (and career) if I wasn't careful.

For the next few months, I was deeply depressed about the real possibility of giving up cross-country racing forever. Then I came up with the only possible solution to my dilemma. Somehow, I convinced my better half to let me switch to UTV racing because side-by-side ("SxS") vehicles have more rider protection (e.g., roll cage, doors, four-point seat belts, etc.). I was happy to "graduate" from a quad to a SxS as long as that meant I could continue XC racing. As they say, with age comes a cage!

When I began racing UTVs in 2015, I quickly realized how drastically different these large vehicles are from ATVs. Both vehicles have their pros and cons, but ATVs are simply more exciting than UTVs. Quads are lighter, more maneuverable, and its rider sits on top of the vehicle with an unimpeded view of the environment around him. On the other hand, UTVs are heavier, less agile, and the riders sit inside a cab that shields them from their surroundings.

Cash & me after one of our first SxS races with TORN.

Soon, I discovered that UTVs offer their own advantages. Compared to quads, side-by-sides are more comfortable, offer better safety features, and provide more ground clearance to handle deep ruts, large boulders, and other obstacles.

Plus, they have cup holders for your beer… just kidding! But the best part of UTVs is having a passenger seat. In a SxS, my teenage son (Cash) can join me as co-pilot while we tackle the race course together. How cool is that?

After a few years of UTV racing in the TORN series (and loving every minute of it except for the long drives), the Texas Off Road Championship Series ("TORCS") announced that it would begin hosting UTV cross-country races in 2017 (see www.torcsracing.com for more info). This was welcome news because TORCS races are located in Central Texas, meaning it would cut my drive time in half.

Like TORN, TORCS is run by wonderful people (Gil "The Punisher" Ramos, his spunky wife, Jackie, and their two sons) who obviously love the sport and do everything possible to make it a fun and safe experience for racers and spectators alike. Solely due to the long distances that I travelled for TORN races, I switched series in February 2017 and have been racing with TORCS ever since.

(from Left to Right) Chad, Dylan, Jackie, & Gil Ramos

Cash has been my co-pilot off and on since I started racing UTVs in 2015, and I have treasured every minute of our time together. Some seasons, he races more than others. In 2019, he participated in less than half of the races. But even when he wasn't able to join me on the track (usually due to unfinished homework), he contributed by helping me wrench on Big Blue or loading and unloading the UTV and equipment on race days. I'm super grateful for all the things Cash has done to support my race efforts!

Before I wrap up this introduction, I want to make one final point about the dedication required for off-road racing. For many people involved in this sport (including myself), racing is far more than just a hobby or something interesting to do from time to time. Many hardcore off-road enthusiasts put their blood, sweat, and wallets into their racing efforts. In addition to the countless hours required for UTV maintenance and race prep (discussed later in this book), this sport requires lots of greenbacks.

Below is a list of typical expenses that are required to compete in SxS racing (excluding the cost of a truck and trailer needed to tow the UTV):

- Cost to purchase a brand-new UTV and install the minimum safety equipment required for off-road racing = $20,000 (give or take a few thousand)

- UTV insurance = $400 per year (optional, but I highly recommend it given the surprising number of SxS thefts that occur every year)

- Regular maintenance, such as replacing motor oil and filter, other fluids, spark plugs, air filter, CVT belt, etc. = $600 per year

- Repairs = $1,000 per year at a minimum (this amount depends on how well the owner maintains the UTV, the age and mileage of the UTV, and how aggressive the driver is)

- Performance upgrades = $2,000 per year (optional, but many types of upgrades can improve race results or add protection, such aftermarket suspension, wheels, tires, motor, clutch, bumpers, roof, skid plates, nerf bars, etc.)

- Race fees = $100 per race ($10 gate fee plus $90 UTV racing fee)

- Fuel cost and road tolls = $100 per race (based on fuel cost and road tolls to travel the 300-mile round trip that Cash and I usually take to each TORCS race, plus fuel for my UTV)

Given the significant financial costs to race (at least $20,000 initial investment plus $6,000 per year) as well as the time commitment required for race prep and travel to and from each event, it is easy to see why most people who participate in this sport are dedicated off-road enthusiasts.

What follows is a recap of my 2019 season competing (with Cash as co-pilot sometimes) in the Turbo SxS class of the TORCS series. Hope you enjoy!

Cash & me at a TORCS race in March 2020.

CHAPTER 1:
Goertz Ranch

On January 27, 2019, I loaded up "Big Blue" (my trusty blue 2018 Polaris RZR XP Turbo) and made the two and one-half hour drive to Goertz Ranch in Rockne, Texas, for Round 1 of the 2019 TORCS series. I was excited that it was finally race day because this was my first opportunity to get some seat time in the RZR since the last race of 2018. Also, I always look forward to racing at Goertz Ranch because this is usually my favorite TORCS track… it's wide and fast!

WHERE:

Rockne, Texas… it's a tiny town about eight miles south of Bastrop. This picturesque property has pecan groves, a few creek crossings, and a large pasture area.

TRACK CONDITIONS:

When I arrived at the track around 1pm, the weather was nice (sunny and mild temps), but the ground was soaking wet thanks to heavy rain the night before. As I pulled into a parking lot, I began to question whether I could find an open parking spot before my two-wheel drive pickup truck got stuck in the mud. Sure enough, I only made it 100 yards past the entrance gate before my rear tires lost traction in the sloppy mud. With a little push from a friendly ATVer (who I never met before), I was quickly on my way to finding a parking spot on high ground next to the track. Turns out, this little challenge getting through the mud was a sign of things to come.

Due to soggy conditions on the track, the TORCS race officials had to re-route the earlier races that day. This delayed our UTV races by an hour. No problem. That's just more time to catch up with my racing buddies, most of whom I haven't seen in a few months.

The track was three miles long and similar to the course we raced on last year at this property, with only a few modifications here and there.

As mentioned above, Cash will sometimes join me as my co-pilot. Unfortunately, he had homework to finish this weekend and that meant I was racing solo this time. However, Cash did take the time to help me prepare for this race, and I know he was with me in spirit during the competition.

RACE PREP:

For those unfamiliar with off-road racing, race prep involves a lot more work than you might think. Here's a brief list of the basic tasks:

- Perform regular maintenance of the UTV plus any repairs needed from the last race
- Pressure washing the UTV (takes two to five hours, depending on whether the last race was dusty or muddy)
- Cleaning helmets, goggles, race suits, gloves, and other equipment
- Cleaning the UTV's air filter
- Re-charging the UTV's battery (e.g., attach a trickle charger between races)
- Blowing the dust off the CVT clutches and belt (I use my leaf blower!)
- Re-filling the gas tank and topping off all other fluids
- Adjusting the tire pressure and shock set-up
- Attaching the trailer to the truck, loading the UTV onto the trailer, and securing it with heavy-duty ratchet straps

- Putting old bed sheets on the seats of the truck and loading the inside of the truck with race equipment, tools, and spare parts (I keep a long list of items that need to be packed on race day)

PARADE LAP & HOT LAP:

Some XC racing series ban practice laps before the competition begins, which forces racers to hit the track cold on Lap 1 at full-speed or at whatever pace they are willing to go. This format is exciting for competitors and spectators alike, but leaves racers prone to mistakes and accidents on the first few laps as they learn the course layout. To reduce these problems and increase safety, some series allow competitors to run practice laps before the race begins, or (alternatively) participate in a parade lap and/or hot lap. The TORCS series allows a parade lap followed by one (optional) hot lap.

Practice laps are just what they sound like and allow racers the opportunity to run the course at any pace they desire for a limited amount of time (e.g., 1 hour). On the other hand, a parade lap is typically comprised of all racers lined up in a single file line and being led slowly around the course by a track official. The parade lap gives racers a good look at the track layout and helps them identify any technical sections (e.g., off-camber trails, steep descents, or other tricky obstacles) as well as pick the best lines whenever alternative trails are provided.

Immediately following the parade lap, TORCS SxS racers are also allowed to run one (optional) hot lap where racers are free to go at their own pace. You might think of a hot lap as a practice lap, but each racer is limited to only one lap instead of a limited period of time. Some racers skip the hot lap and instead use that opportunity to grab their preferred position on the starting line. I always run the hot lap because I believe that the more familiar I am with the course layout, the faster I'll run and the less likely I'll make a critical error on Lap 1 (e.g., make a wrong turn and get passed by several racers behind me).

When it finally came time to start the parade lap around 3:30pm, we had 17 side-by-sides gathered near the starting line. The ground was soft and mushy everywhere, so it was obvious that we were all about to take a huge mud bath.

When the parade lap started, I got in line near the front and followed the line of cars slowly around the muddy course. As always, I was trying to locate any dangerous spots to be aware of during the race and find the best lines wherever alternate routes were available. Of course, the entire track was covered in gooey mud and felt super slippery around turns, so maintaining visibility and traction were the biggest challenges.

In one spot in the woods, the slippery track ran alongside a deep creek. It would not take much to slide off into the water if you weren't careful. In other challenging spots, racers had to cross creeks that were already a sloppy mess and pass through open gates bordered by steel pipes that you didn't want to tangle with.

Photo Credit: Mary Parkinson

CLASSES:

On this outing, there were only three UTVs lined up on the starting line of the Turbo SxS class, including Collin Huber's black RZR Turbo, my blue RZR turbo, and Dwayne Sanders' black Can-Am X3. Noticeably absent from the Turbo line-up was Bubba Gray (last year's champ). Sadly, this was a much smaller turnout than normal. But on the bright side, we were all guaranteed a podium finish (assuming we actually finish the race)!

Behind us were 11 side-by-sides in the Non-turbo class, and they were lined up on two separate lines with staggered start times.

Behind them were three buggies in the 800cc class.

THE START:

The starting area was in a pasture adjacent to the muddy parking area. From the starting line, we had approximately 40 feet to the first left turn around a flagpole.

When the green flag finally when up, I quickly turned the key, but nothing happened. Ugh! Then I tried the key again and got it moving, but not before Collin had already left the starting line. I jumped in behind him and Dwayne fell in behind me. Not a great start, but I knew we had a long race ahead of us and there would be plenty of opportunities to take the lead if I drove smart and stayed out of trouble.

LAPS 1-4:

As our class zig-zagged our way through the big trees in the pasture area, I found myself sliding all over the place. The most obvious challenge was to drive fast and still maintain full control. It would be easy to spin out or slide into a tree. Following close on the heels of Collin's RZR led to the next biggest challenge for me… trying to see the track while eating his roost. For that reason, I backed off a tad so I could see better and avoid getting my goggles (and radiator) packed with mud.

Near the end of this first pasture area, the course makes a 180-degree, left-hand turn and points racers back towards the parking area. That turn was slippery as owl "you know what." Turns out, that was my favorite corner on the track because I could go in hot, simultaneously hit the brakes and turn the steering wheel, then nail the gas pedal and sling-shot around the turn. Fun Stuff!

Next, the course takes you to a fast, wide, straightaway along the edge of the parking lot. Near the end of this short run, I noticed 51 mph on my speedo before I had to make a sharp left turn and then duck through an open gate lined by steel posts.

After that, the course takes riders into the wooded trails that are dotted with pecan trees, muddy creek crossings, and lots of sloppy mud at every turn. I tried to keep Collin within eyesight, but it was challenging to maintain fast speeds and also stay on course. Just one overshot turn could spell disaster and end your day of racing.

When the course exited the woods, it took racers near the pasture area again with more zig-zag turns around large trees. Next, racers crossed through another open gate at a 45-degree angle, made a hard right turn, and ran along the fence line. Next, racers dropped off into another muddy creek crossing, then snaked around a few more turns before ending up near the scoring chute/starting line area. At this point, I was 20 seconds behind Collin. I didn't want to push myself too hard and make a mistake that could end my race early, so I pressed on at my own pace.

A few laps later, I ran up on my first lapper (a slower rider) from the 800cc class. He didn't pull over, so I hugged his rear tires until I found a safe place to pass him on the inside of a left-hand turn and then proceeded onward. The next few lappers I came across pulled aside and let me go around easily.

Unbeknownst to me, Collin got a little too friendly with a fence post near the second gate opening and broke a rear axle around the fourth lap. As a result, he pulled out of the race, and I took the lead. At the time, I had no clue about his whereabouts and was still in hot pursuit for his RZR the rest of the race.

As a side note, it is quite common for side-by-sides to roll-over, hit a tree, or suffer a mechanical break-down during a race. I've participated in some races where almost half of the competitors didn't finish due to driver error, mechanical failure, or just bad luck. By the last lap, the entire course was littered with broken or wrecked UTVs sitting on the side of the trails. In fact, some break down on the track and become a new obstacle to maneuver around. Ugh. Sometimes, winning means just finishing the race.

Photo Credit: Mary Parkinson

SECOND HALF OF THE RACE:

Later in the race, I ran through the scoring chute and heard someone behind me in the near distance. I didn't know who it was, but I figured it must be someone from the Non-turbo class that caught up to me. I pressed on and tried to keep an eye out for him with the intention of letting him pass whenever he got close. There's no point in blocking his progress as we are not in the same class.

So now I'm flying through the slippery, zig zag field towards my favorite 180-degree turn. I planned to go in hot, do a quick 180 spin, and sling-shot around like I normally do, but this time I took a peek in my mirror just as I hit the start of that turn. I didn't see anyone behind me, so I thought I had plenty of room to make the turn.

As I swing around the turn, I suddenly take a hard hit from my left side. Turns out that Cory Williams from the Non-turbo class accidentally bumped me. Oh crap! I never saw him. All I knew was that my steering suddenly felt super hard to turn, and I immediately thought my race was done. I let off the gas for a second and then tried to get in line behind Cory. But it was tough to keep up with him while my steering was out of whack. I immediately jumped to conclusions and thought my tie rods were bent or my front wheels were knocked way out of alignment.

After continuing down the track another 100 yards or so, it occurred to me that perhaps my power steering was malfunctioning as a result of the contact with Cory. To test this theory, I slowed down to reset it (by restarting the engine) and then the steering returned to normal. What a relief! Now I could get back to the business of racing.

As the race continued, I started noticing more and more UTVs broke down along the side of the course. I nearly became a victim myself as I came around one of the slippery turns in the woods where it runs alongside a deep creek. Just as I made a right-hand turn around a big tree, my rear end spins out and now I'm facing backwards on the track! I was relieved that I didn't slide off into the creek, but still concerned about getting straightened out before another racer came around that corner. So, I hit reverse and quickly got back on course.

On Lap 8, my radiator became totally clogged with mud. That caused my engine to overheat and automatically slowed down to crawling speed. Ugh! I had no choice but to pull off the trail for a 30-second cooling break. Then, I cranked it up and ran the course at a much slower pace. I continued to battle overheating troubles for the rest of the race, so I took it easy around the track and pulled over to let other racers pass me whenever they got close.

RACE RESULTS:

After nine sloppy laps, I finally saw the checkered flag and headed back to the trailer. A few seconds later, I saw Collin pull up in his damaged RZR. That's when I discovered he exited the race early, and I ended up finishing first in our class. Dwayne completed eight laps and took second place, and Collin finished third.

Collin Huber & me on the podium at Goertz Ranch

But this adventure was far from over. After loading up Big Blue onto the trailer and collecting my First Place plaque and $50 cash winnings, I still had to exit the parking area without getting my truck stuck. I opted to exit the other way around the parking area instead of the way I came in. But I didn't make it far before my truck started to sink into the mud and my truck tires lost traction. Grrr.

At this point, it was getting dark, so time was of the essence to get unstuck. I quickly unloaded my RZR from the trailer and found someone in the parking area with a UTV. I asked him to pull my trailer backwards and free me from the mud. At one point, this good Samaritan and I were both lying in the mud and using our cell phones for light while we searched for a place to tie his winch cable to my truck's front end. Finally, he freed me from that mudhole, and I was able to proceed towards the exit gate.

Next, my truck made it several more feet through the muddy parking area until I got stuck again. Son of a (beeeeep)! Feeling desperate, I enlisted the help of my rescuer yet again. Sadly, we repeated this stuck-unstuck situation a few more times until he finally pulled my truck and trailer all the way through the exit gate and up the adjoining hill. I gave my new friend most of my race winnings and thanked him for his help. As I've said before, I've met the friendliest people while racing in TORCS and other off-road series, and this guy was no exception.

The last part of this great adventure was the five-plus hours (not kidding!) that it took me to pressure wash the mud off my UTV, truck, trailer, and then driveway. Ugh. The sticky stuff was everywhere and difficult to clean. But it was well worth it for all the fun I had on the race course.

Believe it or not, my 2018 Polaris RZR XP Turbo is under there somewhere.

KNESEK RANCH FEB 23 & 24

SATURDAY

7AM-4:45PM Registration

5pm WOMENS PARADE LAP
then 30 minute race

Gate Fee $10
(under 6 over 60 free)
Camping $10 per night
Saturday Race Fee $50
Sunday Race Fee $90
Membership $45
Transponder $10

GATE HOURS
Friday 5-11pm– gates locked
Sat 6:30am-9pm-gates locked
Sun 7am-3pm

SUNDAY PAYOUT
$50 To Each Sunday Class Winner +
Overall Payout
1-20 1st $120 2nd $80
21-30 1st $200 2nd $120 3rd $80
31-40 1st $280 2nd 210 3rd $140 4th $70

Classes: TURBO, NON TURBO, 800, WOMEN

Race updates will be pushed through the TORCS app created by Thomas Sell
Please download the app and allow push notifications
Check website News Story or TORCS app before you haul!

 TORCS   TORCSRACING   TORCS

SUNDAY

7:30-2:15 Registration

2:30PM RIDERS MEETING
PARADE LAP
Followed by HOT LAP
then 60 min RACE

From Austin take Hwy 79 to
Thorndale, go about 6 miles
to the SECOND CR 434 you
see (it is a loop, do not turn
on the first CR 434 you see)
turn L go 2.5 miles ranch
will be on left. From Houston take 79 to Rockdale,
from Main St in Rockdale
go about 6 miles to CR 434
turn R go 2.5 miles ranch will
be on left
2602 County Road 434 Loop
Rockdale, TX

CHAPTER 2:
Knesek Ranch

On February 24, 2019, I loaded up Big Blue and drove to Knesek Ranch in Rockdale, Texas, for Round 2 of the 2019 TORCS series. In typical "Mike Kowis" fashion, I waited until Sunday morning at 8:30am to begin installing a new front bumper on Big Blue. That simple task took much longer than I expected, and I didn't leave the house till 11:20am. Despite the 50-minute late start, I made it to the track with just enough time to sign up and race. Whew!

WHERE:

Rockdale, Texas… it's a small town approximately 40 miles west of College Station. This property is relatively flat and covered with tons of mesquite trees and cactus (boys and girls, can you say "tire hazards"?) plus a large pasture area. I've raced on this track the last few years with TORCS and always enjoyed it, especially the fast straightaway section near the back of the pasture area.

TRACK CONDITIONS:

When I arrived at the track on Sunday around 1:45pm, the weather was absolutely gorgeous (sunny and 60 degrees). Luckily, the constant rain we had last week at my house didn't materialize much at this location, so the ground was mostly dry. A dry track was a welcome treat for those of us who survived the muddy Round 1 event. A month had passed, and I was still cleaning dirt out of crevices in Big Blue and me. Ugh!

The track was three miles long and similar to the course we had last year at this property.

MISSING CO-PILOT:

Sadly, Cash chose to stay home on Sunday and do his homework instead of being my co-pilot. And by "homework," I mean he stayed home to play games on his new PlayStation 4 gaming console that he bought with his own money. Oh well, I hope he joins me for the next race because I could really use a counterweight… errr, I mean because I would really enjoy spending quality father-son time together.

PARADE LAP & HOT LAP:

When the parade lap started around 2:30pm, we had two dozen side-by-sides gathered near the starting line.

When the parade lap got rolling, I jumped in near the front and followed the line of cars slowly around the course. This track is fairly straightforward with no serious hazards or difficult technical areas to worry about. The first mile was fast and wide and took racers through an open pasture with a few hard 180-degree turns and chicanes ("S" curves) to slow them down from time to time. There was plenty of passing room here if racers can somehow see their way through the thick dust. The remaining two miles consisted of tight, wooded trails through thorny mesquite trees and cactus patches with very few places to pass safely. These wooded trails contained soft soil that eventually turned into deep ruts on parts of the track, especially in the turns (boys and girls, can you say "flipping hazard"?).

Photo Credit: Mary Parkinson

CLASSES:

I was happy to see our Turbo SxS class grow to seven UTVs this race. Behind us were 13 side-by-sides in the Non-turbo class and four buggies in the 800cc class.

My one and only goal for this race was to have fun… okay, who was I kidding? I also wanted to get on the podium. I knew that goal would not be easy with seven of us in the Turbo SxS class and Big Blue still had stock wheels and suspension. I desperately needed to upgrade these components if I want to be competitive this year. So, my plan was to upgrade these items as soon as I could afford them.

THE START:

The starting area was in the large pasture near the edge of the woods. From the starting line, we had approximately 40 feet to the first 90-degree right turn around a flag pole.

31

When I pulled up to the line for my class, I noticed something odd. My gas gauge was only ¾ full. In my haste to get Big Blue loaded onto the trailer this weekend, I only filled up the tank till it read "full" on the gas gauge instead of filling it until it almost spills over. That turned out to be a mistake because now I was concerned about having sufficient fuel to last the entire race.

When the green flag finally went up, I got a lousy start and found myself in fifth position around the first turn. A poor start in this race meant I'd be eating lots of dust as we made our way around the dry pasture area. At this point, I laid back a little and tried my best to avoid hitting anyone in front of me who may be hidden by the thick dust clouds.

LAP 1:

As our class zig-zagged through the pasture area, I found myself on the heels of a Can-Am X3 driven by Donovan Willis. At this point, I decided to just keep up with him. Making a pass here would put me in danger of hitting trees, getting a flat tire, etc. We had a long race ahead of us, so I settled in and stayed focused.

Near the end of this pasture area, the course squeezes through a small chicane that slowed riders down a bit and made them get into a single-file line. Then it was a long straightaway for a few hundred yards till we hit a hard 90-degree left turn. I looked down at one point in the race and hit 73 mph on the speedo at the end of this section. Yee haw!

After making that hard left turn, the course takes racers back through another straightaway where I quickly hit 66 mph before slamming on the brakes to make a hard 180 turn and follow the trail along the edge of the woods. At this point, the trail has a dip and then a small jump. Every time I hit this jump, I could feel all four wheels come off the ground. It felt just like a roller coaster. What a rush!

The trail then took racers around a sweeping left-hand turn at 40 mph and dumped them into the wooded section. The next two miles were an exercise in tree dodging or "threading the needle" as I sometimes call it. My stock tires (29" tall) and stock suspension made Big Blue feel top-heavy on these turns and tended to put me up on two wheels if I was too hot into the corners. This was yet another reminder to upgrade parts on my RZR in the near future.

At the end of Lap 1, I was only a few seconds behind Donovan and could see him just ahead of me in the open pasture area. So, I pressed onward hoping to pass him at some point later in the race. Again, the dust made it a challenge to get close to him in this wide-open section and the wooded section was too narrow to pass safely. So, my options were a bit limited. But I pressed on anyway in hopes of finding a way around him.

Photo Credit: Mary Parkinson

SECOND HALF OF THE RACE:

Later in the race, the ruts in the woods got deeper and I started seeing more and more UTVs broken down or flipped onto their sides. That was a stark reminder that I needed to keep my speed in check and avoid the flipping over or nailing a tree.

At one point in the pasture area, I made a hard 180-degree left turn, which pointed me towards a second 180-degree (right) turn just a short distance ahead. As I made my way around that first 180 turn, I kept my foot on the gas. However, my front tires were pushing and I ended up going wide around this turn and headed towards oncoming traffic. Yikes! I slammed on the brakes and turned back into my lane to avoid a racer that was headed towards me. Oh boy, that could have been ugly.

At another point in the pasture section, I found myself sliding around a hard left turn. Suddenly, Big Blue's right two tires gained traction and it rose up on its right side. I quickly counter-steered to avoid flipping over. Just then, I noticed a nearby spectator raise his fist in the air as if to say, "Good job!" I smiled and waved back as if to say, "Yeah, I meant to do that. Enjoy the show, folks! I'll be here all week." In reality, that was a scary moment; and I'm thankful that my bladder wasn't full at the time of this little stunt.

As the race progressed, I continued to follow Donovan's X3 and could easily see him whenever we reached the open pasture area. At that point, I was starting to get passed by some of the faster Non-turbo cars, which were led by Ken Asklund and his Yamaha UTV displaying the number 1 plates (meaning he won the championship in his class last season). I tried to get out of their way whenever I saw them approaching. Generally, I could hold them off easily in the pasture area, but Big Blue was no match for them in the tight, twisty woods.

At one point, I caught up to an 800cc buggy near the end of the wooded trails. Instead of trying to pass him there, I waited until the course pops out of the woods and makes a wide, sweeping left turn near the parking area and then drops back into the woods. As soon as I reached this turn, I took the inside lane and hit the gas. I easily got around him and then I heard a "honk." That was odd. Why would he honk at me? For one thing, we are not in the same class, so it doesn't matter if I pass him. Also, I would think he would be relieved to finally get me off his tail. Oh well, I pressed onward.

LAPS 10 and 11:

It's now the tenth lap, and there are a half-dozen UTVs broke down all over the track. I'm still behind Donovan's X3. And then it happens. Big Blue started sputtering on hard right-hand turns in the pasture area. What was that? I've never heard that sound before or felt it lose power on turns. Then I checked the fuel gauge. Only one bar left. Holy Toledo, Batman! At that point, I could just hope and pray that I would somehow make it to the end of that lap. Then I started getting more worried. What if I run out of gas in the middle of the tight woods and block the course?

Finally, I made it to the scoring chute. But wait, there's no checkered flag! That meant I had another three miles to go. At this point, I'm really nervous. The gauge is still on one bar and it's starting to sputter more often on sharp right turns (which means the fuel level was so low that it sloshes away from the side of the gas tank where the fuel line draws in fuel for the engine). At this point, all I could do was pray that I'd make it to the end.

Me celebrating another podium finish.

RACE RESULTS:

Woo hoo! I was so relieved to finally see the checkered flag that I didn't stop to chat with my fellow racers near the finish line. Instead, I headed straight for the trailer before I ran out of fumes. Thanks to a few folks in my class who either flipped onto their side or broke down (like Collin's RZR that blew a belt mid-race), I ended up taking third place behind Donovan Willis (second) and Bubba Gray (first). It was great race, and I was thrilled to get a podium finish after nearly running out of fuel and avoiding a near collision in the pasture area.

37

CHAPTER 3:
OTT Ranch

I was excited about racing at Ott Ranch on April 7, 2019, but Mother Nature had different plans. She brought heavy downpours on the morning of this race. As soon as it became evident that our scheduled race was no longer safe for racers and spectators, the TORCS officials made the right call by cancelling the event. Unfortunately, I didn't get word of this decision until I was already halfway to the track. This meant that I had to turn around on heavily-congested Interstate 10 and drive back through the turbulent weather that I had just passed through. The weather was so intense that traffic was barely moving along this interstate highway at 20 mph. Ugh! It was stressful driving for sure, but I made it home safely an hour or so later. On the bright side, at least I didn't have to clean any mud off my RZR when I got home.

OTT RANCH 2.0
APRIL 27 & 28
STI

SATURDAY
7AM-4:45PM Registration
5pm WOMENS PARADE LAP,
Hot Lap then 30 minute race

Gate Fee $10
(under 6 over 60 free)
Camping $10 per night
Saturday Race Fee $50
Sunday Race Fee $90
Membership $45
Transponder $10

GATE HOURS
Friday 5-11pm– gates locked
Sat 6:30am-9pm-gates locked
Sun 7am-3pm

100%

SUNDAY PAYOUT
$50 To Each Sunday Class Winner +
Overall Payout
1-20 1st $120 2nd $80
21-30 1st $200 2nd $120 3rd $80
31-40 1st $280 2nd 210 3rd $140 4th $70

Classes:TURBO, NON TURBO, 800, WOMEN

Race updates will be pushed through the TORCS app created by Thomas Sell
Please download the app and allow push notifications

Check website News Story or TORCS app before you haul!

SUNDAY
7:30-2:15 Registration
2:30PM RIDERS MEETING
PARADE LAP
Followed by HOT LAP
then 60 min RACE

Austin: Hwy-71 towards
Bastrop to TX-304. Turn R onto TX-304 and go about 20
miles to Cedar Rock Road/CR
285, turn L into entrance.
Houston: I-10 to TX –304
turn R onto TX-304 follow
for about 14 miles to Cedar
Rock Road/CR285, turn R into
entrance
4205 S HWY 304, Rosanky,
TX 78953
512-632-2369

f TORCS   TORCSRACING   YouTube TORCS

39

CHAPTER 4:
OTT Ranch 2.0

On April 28, 2019, I loaded up Big Blue and drove to OTT Ranch in Rosanky, Texas, for Round 4 of the 2019 TORCS series. Unlike the last round, the Mother Nature cooperated this time and the race proceeded as planned. I was looking forward to this race because I just upgraded Big Blue with new wheels and tires that should improve its handling characteristics.

WHERE:

Rosanky, Texas… it's a tiny speck on the map located about 20 miles south of Bastrop. This picturesque property had a nice mix of thick woods and open pastures.

TRACK CONDITIONS:

When I arrived at OTT Ranch at 1pm, the weather was warm and sunny with a comfortable, cool breeze. What a GREAT day for racing! This property has lots of sandy soil and the small amount of rain that fell earlier in the week wasn't enough to knock down much of the dust on race day. That meant trying to see the course through thick dust was Challenge Number One on this track.

The track was three miles long, and most of it ran through very tight, wooded trails. About halfway through the course, the track took racers onto a large pasture area with long, sweeping turns that zig-zag back and forth. During the race, I was hitting 48 mph going into the first right-hand turn in the pasture… fun stuff!

PARADE LAP & HOT LAP:

When the parade lap started around 2:30pm, 20 side-by-sides gathered near the starting line.

Once the parade lap got rolling, I jumped in the front of the line to avoid some of the thick dust. But then I quickly pulled over and stopped to change from Low to High gear. Doh! I hopped back in line and then proceeded slowly around the course.

The first thing I noticed was how much tighter this course is when compared to other TORCS races. It was stressful driving through the tight sections. In fact, my butt was clinched so tight to the seat that I probably didn't need a seat belt.

Racing through tight woods is not my favorite, but it normally doesn't scare me. What does scare me is racing through tight woods with a brand-new set of tires and wheels that have a wider offset than stock. Looks like I picked the wrong race to try out my new shoes on Big Blue. Doh!

The first mile of this course ran through the woods with a few spots that were extra snug. In fact, the bark was already rubbed off the insides of some of the trees. Because of my wider wheel stance (which I was not yet used to), I decided to stick my head out the left side of the RZR to make sure that my front left tire cleared the trees. Despite the obvious danger, I did this a few more times during the race until I finally felt comfortable that my front tires would clear the trees.

The next time I decide to add wider tires and wheels, I will do myself a favor and get some seat time on the car before racing it. Sticking my head out of the window during a race through the woods was not the smartest thing I've ever done.

After the first mile, the course took racers into a large open pasture on what appeared to be freshly-graded soil across the entire field. There was no grass here, so dust would obviously be an obstacle to overcome.

After the large pasture area, the trail ran next to an old farmhouse on the far side of the field and then ducked between the trees for another quarter mile of zig-zag, wooded trails before hitting a long, wide, straight section. During the race, I put my foot down in this section and hit speeds of 63 mph before slamming on the brakes at the end and turning right into the woods again. Like the first part of the course, the trails were very tight here, and I had to be on guard to avoid the trees.

At one point, the trail makes a left and goes downhill through a dry creek and then climbs back up the other side. This section was wide, fast, and a little bumpy, but lots of fun like a roller coaster. Spectators were lined up along the left side of the hill climb area to watch and take pics, which made it a bit scary because the bumps caused Big Blue to bounce all over the trail as I zoomed past them. Luckily, I never came close to the crowds, but the danger crossed my mind every time.

After the hill climb, the track made a 90-degree right turn into the woods. Not far up the trail, it made a sharp left turn that was tight and a bit tricky. During the parade lap, I started the turn too close to the inside of this turn and had to stop and back up to get through it. During the race, I got stuck behind a bottleneck after another racer had the same trouble and he eventually had to be pushed off the track (his UTV apparently broke down).

Near the last part of the course, the trail runs along a barbed-wife fence that separates the wooded trails from the parking area. This section was fast and straight. Afterwards, it made a sharp left turn, ran through a dry creek bottom, and then popped out near the scoring chute where the next lap began.

Because this property was covered in soft soil, the track quickly formed two deep ruts all the way around. That meant Challenge Number Two would be avoiding getting hung up in the deep ruts. In other words, racers must avoid being high-centered in the ruts or flipping over in the tight turns.

Challenge Number Three would be finding a safe place to pass. With so many tight woods and deep ruts, it would not be easy to get around slower racers unless they pulled off the trail.

CLASSES:

Four UTVs signed up for the Turbo SxS class, but only three made it to the starting line after my buddy Collin busted a ball joint during the parade lap. Collin is a good competitor, so I was disappointed to see him drop out of the race. Hopefully, his bad luck will turn around at the next one, and he can give our class a run for the money. With Collin out, that left two Can-Am X3s and me on the front line. On the plus side, I was guaranteed a podium finish as long as I completed the race.

Behind our class were a dozen side-by-sides in the Non-turbo class, followed by four buggies in the 800cc class.

STRATEGY:

With so many tight trails and lots of dust on the track, winning the holeshot would be a huge advantage towards winning this race. In other words, whoever takes the lead around the first turn puts himself in the position of racing on a clean track and forces his competitors to battle through a dusty course. I figured that all I had to do was beat both X3s to the first turn and then I had a decent shot at taking home the gold. Sitting on the starting line, I was ready and determined to make that happen.

THE START:

The starting area was in a large pasture near the edge of the woods. From the starting line, we had approximately 50 feet to the first left turn around a pole. Then the trail snaked left and right before dumping into the woods on the left side. Before the flag man called our attention, I hit the starter one last time to make sure it was ready to fire up. But the motor hesitated and then started up. That was weird! I hadn't noticed it hesitate like that before. Uh oh, now I'm really nervous. Would I beat the X3s to the first turn?

When the green flag finally when up, I hit the key and the starter spun over.

But the motor didn't fire up. What? Nooooo!

As I hit the key again, I watched in S-L-O-W motion as both X3s made their way towards turn number one without me moving at all. When my competitors were halfway to the first turn, Big Blue finally roared to life. Ugh! My heart sank as I quickly took my place in last position around the first turn behind Dwayne Sanders (currently in the lead) and Brian Schroeder (in second position). At this point, I knew it was going to be a long, grueling race.

LAPS 1 and 2:

As our class zig-zagged our way through the tight woods, I stayed on Brian's tail and he was right behind Dwayne. The three of us made our way together through the course and completed the first lap in that same order.

Somewhere on the second lap, Brian passed Dwayne while I was still running in third position.

On the second lap where we approached the big open pasture area, Cory Williams and another Non-turbo racer caught up to me. I pulled over and let them both pass me as we entered the pasture area. Now I'm eating the dust of four UTVs, which made it very challenging to see the course and keep up my speed. I dropped back a little to get some clean air with the hope that I could catch up after the Non-turbo cars finally got around the X3s ahead of me.

Soon after we left the pasture area on the second lap, Dwayne pulled off to the left side and let me pass him on the fast, straight section. So now I took over second position behind Brian. One down and one to go!

Photo Credit: Mary Parkinson

LAPS 3 through 9:

As the race continued, the ruts got deeper and deeper. Then I started seeing more UTVs broken down or flipped onto their sides. I would come around a corner and suddenly see a UTV on its side with the driver standing next to it signaling me to be cautious. Whenever I saw this, I would slow down and yell out the window to ask if they were okay. Once I heard or could see that they were safe, I would hit the gas and continue onward.

After a few more laps, I started getting more comfortable driving at a faster clip through the tight woods and only slowed down a little for the super tight places where tree bark was missing. At one point, the trail hits a section where it squeezes racers through a narrow opening between two trees. I hit that section a bit too fast on one lap and my RZR seemed to slide out of the ruts towards one of the two trees. Yikes! I only missed the tree by an inch or two. Going forward, that near miss caused me to check my speed whenever I hit that section.

As the race progressed, another racer from the Non-turbo class caught me, and I let him pass as soon as I could do so in a safe place. I continued pushing hard with the hope of catching Brian. The only UTVs that I recall passing were a few slower buggies from the 800cc class.

On one of the last few laps, I entered the woods following the fast, straight section where I ran up on a Non-turbo racer that was high-centered on a left turn. Luckily, I was able to squeeze around him and keep going. Seeing that unlucky guy stuck in the deep ruts caused me to re-focus my attention on keeping my speed up whenever I approached deep ruts so that I didn't end up like him.

Photo Credit: Mary Parkinson

RACE RESULTS:

When I finally reached the checkered flag, I finished in second place. Congrats to Brian Schroeder for taking the win (he was a minute and 10 seconds ahead of me), Dwayne Sanders for taking third, and everyone else who finished this grueling race. Next time, I'll try to improve my start and maybe I'll get better results.

SPOAKS MX
JUNE 8 & 9

SATURDAY
7AM-4:45PM Registration
5pm WOMENS PARADE LAP,
Hot Lap then 30 minute race

Gate Fee $10
(under 6 over 60 free)
Camping $10 per night
Saturday Race Fee $50
Sunday Race Fee $90
Membership $45
Transponder $10

GATE HOURS
Friday 5-11pm– gates locked
Sat 6:30am-9pm-gates locked
Sun 7am-3pm

SUNDAY PAYOUT
$50 To Each Sunday Class Winner +
Overall Payout
1-20 1st $120 2nd $80
21-30 1st $200 2nd $120 3rd $80
31-40 1st $280 2nd 210 3rd $140 4th $70

Classes:TURBO, NON TURBO, 800, WOMEN

Race updates will be pushed through the TORCS app created by Thomas Sell
Please download the app and allow push notifications
Check website News Story or TORCS app before you haul!

SUNDAY
7:30-2:15 Registration
2:30PM RIDERS MEETING
PARADE LAP
Followed by HOT LAP
then 60 min RACE

1930 Barth RD,
Lockhart, TX 7864
512-632-2369

 TORCS TORCSRACING TORCS

CHAPTER 5:
Spoaks MX

On June 9, 2019, I loaded up Big Blue and drove to Spoaks MX in Lockhart, Texas, for Round 5 of the 2019 TORCS series. I was excited to compete in this race because I finally brought my secret weapon...Cash!

Having a co-pilot can be advantageous for a number of reasons, including:

- Having a warm body in the passenger seat provides a counter-balance to help keep the UTV on all four wheels when making sharp turns.

- A co-pilot can point out danger spots or sudden turns ahead, which comes in handy when the driver sometimes gets tunnel vision and only sees the trail immediately in front of the car.

- A co-pilot can point out faster racers who approach from behind. This information is important because it usually means the driver should let the faster UTV pass at the next safe place if the faster racer is not in the same class. Alternatively, if the faster racer is in the same class, then the driver needs to decide whether to pick up the pace or be prepared for a pass from the faster racer if you don't pull over.

- Sharing the race experience with a co-pilot makes the event so much more fun than going it alone.

- Having your family member as your co-pilot creates lasting memories and draws them closer together. Even if this was the only benefit, I'd still prefer having my son as co-pilot.

WHERE:

Lockhart, Texas… it's a small town (known as the "BBQ Capital of Texas") located 30 miles south of Austin. This race was held on a MX track that is surrounded by mesquite trees and cow pastures.

TRACK CONDITIONS:

When we raced on this property last year, the ground was extremely muddy. This year's race was the exact opposite, meaning the conditions were hot and dry. The bone dry and loose sandy soil meant that racers would have to battle through thick dust clouds to see their way to the finish line. The other big challenge here was staying hydrated in the summertime temps, which were in the mid-90s for this race. For that reason, I'm glad that Cash and I stopped on the way to the track to pick up a new camelback for my son (to replace his old leaky one).

The track was 4.5 miles long and contained a nice mixture of terrain. We ran the track in the opposite direction of last year's race. The first mile and a half ran through twisty, wooded trails. Next, the course took racers into a large open field that alternated between fast straights and either sharp or sweeping turns. When racers exited the pasture area through an open gate, the course made a 180-degree left turn and then proceeded through another mile of woods. Finally, the course popped onto the motocross ("MX") track, which included a small whoops section, a tabletop jump, and lots of left and right turns before reaching the scoring chute.

PARADE LAP & HOT LAP:

When the parade lap started at 2:30pm, 20 side-by-sides gathered near the starting line.

Once the parade lap got underway, Cash and I jumped in line behind the lead car as it headed into the first woods section. Even at a slow pace, thick dust made it a challenge to see where we were going. For that reason, we tried to keep a little distance between the lead car and us so we could see the course.

My initial impression was that this course was wide and fast, which is my favorite kind of race! If it wasn't so darn dusty, it would be super fast.

In the first section of woods, there was a smooth trail that felt like a roller coaster. Basically, the trail comes over a small hill and then drops down a few feet before coming back up again. When you hit it at a fast pace, your tires felt like they came off the ground. Cash later told me this was his favorite part of the course, and I felt the same way.

My other impression was that the MX track was very confusing. The course skipped some of the bigger MX jumps and obstacles, but included others. At one point during the parade lap, the lead car and I took the outside line around a tree and quickly discovered that we both ran off the marked course. A few cars behind us took the correct route (inside the tree) and we jumped back in line behind them.

Near the end of the MX section, the course is supposed to take racers between two trees adjacent to a medium-sized jump. I wasn't sure where to go and decided to roll over the jump at a slow pace. Cash immediately pointed out my error and reminded me to avoid that jump every lap thereafter.

CLASSES:

For this race, a pair of Textron Wildcat XX UTVs driven by experienced UTV racers (Blake Gustin and Michael Dunnagan) showed up to join the fun. For some strange reason, the TORCS officials put them in the Turbo SxS class, even though their cars were naturally aspirated (Non-turbo). So, the Turbo SxS class had a total of six UTVs, including the two Textron Wildcats, a pair of RZR Turbos, plus a pair of Can-Am X3s. In addition, 10 UTVs showed up for the Non-turbo class and three buggies ran in the 800cc class.

STRATEGY:

With so much dust on this course, taking an early lead in the race would be a huge advantage. With that in mind, my hope was to get Big Blue started and moving off the line quickly. At the last race, my RZR's engine turned over and over and over before it finally fired up, leaving me in last position around turn number one. Unfortunately, Big Blue was acting up again right before the start of this race too. Sometimes, it would not turn over at all when I hit the key, and other times it turned over, but didn't fire up instantly. At this point, I suspected a weak battery, but wasn't sure. Perhaps I forgot to push on the brake pedal. I just don't know. All I knew for sure was that I lost confidence in my machine and that in and of itself was bad news.

THE START:

The starting area was located between the MX track and the first woods section. From the starting line, racers headed straight towards a few large trees before making a slight right turn onto a dirt trail that led into the woods. As I recall, I was in the middle of the starting line with Collin Huber (black RZR Turbo) to my immediate left and a Can-Am to his left. The rest of the Turbo SxS class was on my right.

After Cash and I joined hands in prayer to ask God to watch over the safety of all competitors, we bumped fists and then got serious about the start of the race (which is our typical pre-race routine). Finally, the flagman pointed to each racer as a signal to ask if we were ready. I nodded my head when he pointed at me and stared directly at his flag with intensity. After he finished going down the row, he stood still for a few seconds and then suddenly waved the green flag high in the air. I turned the key as quickly as I could and, and, and…

Nothing happened. Ugh!

I turned the key all the way off and then tried it again. This time it came to life and off I went. This split-second delay was just enough to give everyone else the jump off the line. As we all raced towards the big trees ahead of us, I noticed that I was near the back of the pack next to the Can-Am X3 on my left. When we reached the trail that leads racers into the woods, Cash and I were in fifth position out of six in our class. Not off to a good start, but it's a long race and anything is possible.

It was so dusty at this point that I almost took the wrong trail that went away from the woods. Doh! For the first quarter mile or so, I repeatedly sped up, got totally lost in the dust clouds, slowed to a crawl until I could see the course again, and then sped up again. This pattern was frustrating, but soon we had enough distance between us and the racer immediately ahead to see the track and keep a steady pace.

LAP 1:

As our class zig-zagged our way through the first section of woods, I maintained as much speed as I could safely go. As we left the woods towards the open pasture area, the course became very wide and super dusty. Suddenly, the thick dust cleared and I could see that the trail made a hard 90-degree turn to the right. Straight ahead was white ribbon to keep racers on the course, but it appeared that someone had already blown through it and went straight. That would be an easy mistake given the clouds of dust everywhere.

After we made the right turn, the trail heads towards a large tree about 200 yards up the trail. I looked down and read 66 mph on the speedo at the end of this stretch. Then the course made a hard left turn and another right where racers hit the longest straight section on the course (where I later hit 71 mph) before slamming on the brakes and making a hard left turn.

With so much dust to slow us down, Cash and I completed Lap 1 with a sluggish lap time of eight minutes and nine seconds (which turned out to be our slowest lap of the race). Despite being 45 seconds behind the leader, we somehow found ourselves in fourth position with a lot of race remaining.

Cash & me after a super dusty race!

LAPS 2 through 8:

Lap 2 was considerably faster as we knocked 30 seconds off our lap time and then continued to race at a seven and one-half minute pace for the rest of the day.

Around Lap 4, Collin broke an axle and pulled out of the race (unbeknownst to Cash and me). On this same lap, Cash handed me the nozzle for my camelback so I could wash down a mouthful of dust that I had just ingested while blazing through the pasture area. As I bit down to draw water, the nozzle fell off the end of the hose and hit the floor. At that point, my camelback no longer worked (couldn't draw water directly from the hose for some reason). Thank goodness Cash raced with me on this day so that I could share his water for the rest of the race. Otherwise, I would have had to head back to the trailer along with Collin. No way I could continue racing in 95-degree heat without water to drink.

Around the fifth lap, I occasionally heard the annoying, high-pitched sound of one of the Textron Wildcats behind me, but I couldn't see him until we hit the large pasture area. At this point, I'm guessing he was about 10 seconds behind us. So, Cash and I pressed onward as fast as possible. As we started Lap 7, the Textron was only a few seconds behind, so I decided to pull over and let him (safely) pass us before we entered the woods. I could have tried to hold him off a little while longer, but didn't want to put him in a situation where he had to work to pass us in the thick dust and potentially cause a wreck.

As the race progressed, Cash and I passed a few UTVs from the 800cc class and we let Ken Asklund from the Non-turbo class pass us as soon as he caught up to us. Near the end of the race, I was guessing that Cash and I were in fourth or fifth position.

Cash & me celebrating another fun race together.

RACE RESULTS:

When Cash and I finally reached the checkered flag, we finished in third place behind both of the Textron Wildcats. Congrats to the Textron racers, Blake Gustin and Michael Dunnagan, for taking home first and second, respectively. They ran a solid race in tough conditions. Next time, I hope to get my starting problem resolved and maybe we'll have better results.

(1st) Blake Gustin, (2nd) Michael Dunnagan,
(3rd) Mike & Cash Kowis, (announcer) Cory Williams

FUN FACT:

The day after this race, my full-time employer hosted a meeting with over 100 employees from the finance department. To kick off this annual event, they selected two employees to speak about their favorite "fun fact" or anything interesting that we do outside of work. I was one of the two employees chosen to speak about my fun fact, which was competing in off-road racing. I was limited to a few minutes, but I could have easily talked for an hour about how much Cash and I enjoy racing with our TORCS brothers and sisters. I hope we can continue to race with this motley group for many years to come.

RUSTY'S
JUNE 29 & 30
STI

Photo courtesy of GraphicsGuysMotorsports.com

SATURDAY
7AM-4:45PM Registration
5pm WOMENS PARADE LAP,
Hot Lap then 30 minute race

Gate Fee $10
(under 6 over 60 free)
Camping $10 per night
Saturday Race Fee $50
Sunday Race Fee $90
Membership $45
Transponder $10

GATE HOURS
Friday 5–11pm– gates locked
Sat 6:30am-9pm-gates locked
Sun 7am-3pm

SUNDAY PAYOUT
$50 To Each Sunday Class Winner +
Overall Payout
1-20 1st $120 2nd $80
21-30 1st $200 2nd $120 3rd $80
31-40 1st $280 2nd 210 3rd $140 4th $70

Classes:TURBO, NON TURBO, 800, WOMEN

Race updates will be pushed through the TORCS app created by Thomas Sell
Please download the app and allow push notifications
Check website News Story or TORCS app before you haul!

SUNDAY
7:30-2:15 Registration
2:30PM RIDERS MEETING
PARADE LAP
Followed by HOT LAP
then 60 min RACE

From Hwy 71 & FM 20 outside
of Bastrop take FM 20 South for
6.2 miles to Pleasant Chapel
Rd, turn R go .02 miles
track will be on left.

394 Pleasant Chapel Rd,
Cedar Creek, TX 78612
512-632-2369

 TORCS TORCSRACING TORCS

57

CHAPTER 6:
Rusty's Walnut Creek

On June 30, 2019, I loaded up Big Blue and drove to Rusty's Walnut Creek for Round 6 of the 2019 TORCS series. This was our last race before the summer break, so I was hoping to finish strong and keep my momentum going. Unfortunately, Cash couldn't join me this time because he was at home recovering from wisdom teeth removal.

WHERE:

Rockne, Texas… it's a small town 30 miles southeast of Austin. The front of this property has a large, grassy pasture for the parking area and lots of woods in the back for the track. I recall racing on this property a few years ago in TORCS's first ever UTV race. I'll never forget that day because it was held on Super Bowl Sunday, and I was worried no one would show up. Fortunately, we had a good turnout that day, and my son and I had a blast in the race! We've been hooked on this series ever since.

TRACK CONDITIONS:

Our last race in early June was scorching hot and the course was blanketed with thick clouds of dust. Luckily, Mother Nature brought us a gift last Saturday night in the form of a few inches of rain to knock down both the heat and dust. Sunday was warm (mid-80s) and partly cloudy, but much more bearable than our last race. The much-needed rain soaked the ground and then some. In fact, the UTV course had several places with slippery mud or standing water.

The track was laid out on 3.7 miles of twisty trails through the woods. Much of the course ran through soft, sandy dirt that eventually turned into deep ruts by the end of the race. The low-lying areas had lots of slippery trails that zig-zagged through the trees.

PARADE LAP & HOT LAP:

When the parade lap started at 2:30pm, 17 side-by-sides gathered near the starting line in a small field near the scoring chute.

As we made our way around the track for the first time, my initial impression was that it was fast and wide, except for one small section of tight trees about midway through the course. Also, there were some seriously slippery sections in the low-lying areas that made it tricky to stay on course, even at moderate speeds. There were only a few safe places to pass, so getting a good start was critical.

Another notable observation was that the last 100 yards of the course ran along a fence line where the trail was completely covered with one foot of water. Hitting this section at moderate speed made a mess of my goggles. And one second after the fresh spray of muddy water hit my helmet, the musty scent of manure overwhelmed my senses. Ugh! Really?

CLASSES:

The turnout for this race was a little less than last time, with only three UTVs in my class. The good news was that everyone in this class gets on the podium as long as we finish the race. The bad news is that anything can happen and no one is guaranteed to make it to the end. In addition, a dozen side-by-sides showed up for the Non-turbo class and two buggies ran in the 800cc class.

STRATEGY:

With plenty of mud and standing water on the track, I used two things to prepare myself for this race.

First, I put several tear-offs on my googles, which are a must have for any mud race. For those unfamiliar, tear-offs are thin sheets of clear or tinted plastic that cover the outer surface of goggles. Whenever one gets dirty, you simply tear it off and reveal a clean one underneath. Hence the name, tear-offs. Many off-road racers stack five or more tear-offs on their goggles right before a muddy race to maintain their vision.

Second, I tried something new to protect my radiator. In past races, mud packed into the fins of my radiator (located right behind the front bumper) and eventually caused overheating problems. To avoid this situation, many UTV racers relocate their radiator to the rear of the vehicle, but I'm still not convinced that this strategy is necessary. Instead, I taped up my front bumper with duct tape to keep most of the mud out of the radiator. I've successfully used this trick on my old ATVs, but this was my first attempt using it on Big Blue.

THE START:

I was lined up in the middle of the starting line with Dwayne Sanders' black Can-Am X3 on my far left and Donovan Willis' red and yellow X3 on my far right. When the green flag appeared, I hit the key and nothing happened. Nooooooooo… not again! The same problem happened during the last few races, and I haven't yet replaced the battery to see if that solves the problem. Doh!

All I could do was watch as Donovan pulled away from the line and left me standing still. I turned the key off and on again and it roared to life this time. I mashed the go pedal and fell in line behind Donovan as we made our way around the first turn to the left. Dwayne was right behind me. Next time, I'll be ready with a new battery. Grrr.

LAP 1:

As our class zig-zagged our way through the first section of woods, I tried to keep Donovan in my sights. I could still see him when we reached the muddy, low-lying area about halfway through the lap, and I felt good about that.

As I hit the zig-zag trails in that area, Big Blue was sliding from one side of the track to the other. It was all I could do to avoid the large trees and still maintain a decent pace.

Near the end of the low-lying area, the trail takes a hard right to go around a watery section of the course. Next, the trail took racers through a wide grassy area that descends to a dry, shallow gully at the bottom. I hit this little dip hard in an effort to keep up with Donovan, and my stock front shocks let me know that was not kosher! Mental note: I need to slow down on that dip for the next lap.

Soon thereafter, the trail eventually goes through a narrow section of trees. This area was the only tight, wooded section and it wasn't too bad as long as you paid close attention.

Not far up the trail, the racers made a hard right into the woods where they cross a short, narrow bridge. This section was slicker than greased owl poop, so I had to be careful to get my RZR pointed straight before I hit the bridge so as not to fall off the edge. A few feet up the trail was another narrow platform, but this one bowed down. When I hit it at moderate speeds during the parade lap and hot lap, it was smooth and fun. But during the race, I picked up the pace and it launched my back end skyward. As I landed, Big Blue bounced all over the track, and I tried my best to stay on course and avoid the trees lined along the edges. These stock shocks are killing me, but I hope to remedy that over the summer.

Near the back half of the course, the track brings racers into a small, open area and eventually makes a few sharp turns through deep ruts and bumps. Afterwards, the trail ran straight about 50 yards and then made a sharp right turn into the woods. As soon as you hit that section, the trail made an awkward 90-degree, right-hand turn over a sizeable bump and onto a trail that is barely wide enough for my tires. It was challenging to make this awkward turn at speed, especially with the large bump immediately before it. I did my best and kept on trucking.

Just happy to have survived another hard fought XC race.

LAPS 2 through 8:

Near the end of my third lap, I hit the water-covered trail near the fence line a little too fast and the aromatic water splashed all over my goggles again. Pee-yew! The nasty water blurred the vision over my left eye, so I started going through the tear-offs until I could see clearly again. Turns out that the nasty water got behind all of the tear-offs, so I had to ditch them all to see again. Ugh! With several laps to go, this was not ideal.

About a mile into Lap 4, I started to hear "Ken and company" (what I call the Non-turbo class) catching up to my rear bumper. Suddenly, I lost power and saw the overheating light display on my dash. Oh crap! I pulled over and let the faster Non-turbo racers pass me. Unlike past mud races when overheating strikes, I had a plan this time. I remained calm, climbed out of Big Blue, and grabbed my utility knife. With a few slashes, I removed the duct tape from my front bumper and dashed back into the RZR. Fifteen minutes later, I was strapped in and ready to go! Okay, this detour only cost me about 90 seconds, but it sure felt like 15 minutes when you see other UTVs passing you. Luckily, I never had another overheating problem for the rest of the race, so this tactic seemed to work well on my RZR.

Turns out, I wasn't the only person who made an emergency pit stop. I later talked to Dwayne at the finish line, and he told me that his lug nuts backed off during the race and his rear wheel got wobbly. So he had to pull over and tighten them. Good thing he noticed that before it became a three-wheeler!

As the race continued, the ground started to dry up and get tacky. Soon, my tires started getting more traction. At one point, I made a sharp left turn around a tree that I had previously slid around. This time, my right tires unexpectedly grabbed and caused my RZR to suddenly pop up on the right two wheels. This would not have been so scary if there was not a big tree directly in front of me. Yikes!

At the last second, Big Blue came back down on all fours, and I steered hard to the left just in time to avoid hitting the tree. What a relief! I dodged a bullet that time.

On the last few laps, I lapped the buggies in the 800c class. I was following one of them (driven by my friend Howard Brown) around a right turn and noticed that he took the turn extra wide. As I made my way around that same turn, I discovered why. The ruts got so deep in the corner that he had to go wide to avoid getting high-centered. Just after that turn, he pulled off to the side and let me pass. Thanks, buddy!

Finished 2nd in this race. Hoping to do better the next time we race here in Round 10.

RACE RESULTS:

When I finally reached the checkered flag, I took home second place in my class and fourth overall. Congrats to Donovan Willis and Dwayne Sanders for taking the win and third place, respectively, in our Turbo SxS class! They both ran a strong race. As for Big Blue, I'm planning a few upgrades over summer and hope to be more competitive when we return to racing in the fall.

COLE'S FUN PIT
SEPT 7 & 8
STI

Photo credit lapkingracing.com

SATURDAY
7AM-4:45PM Registration
5pm WOMENS PARADE LAP,
Hot Lap then 30 minute race

Gate Fee $10
(under 6 over 60 free)
Camping $10 per night
Saturday Race Fee $50
Sunday Race Fee $90
Membership $45
Transponder $10

GATE HOURS
Friday 5-11pm– gates locked
Sat 6:30am-9pm-gates locked
Sun 7am-3pm

SUNDAY PAYOUT
$50 To Each Sunday Class Winner +
Overall Payout
1-20 1st $120 2nd $80
21-30 1st $200 2nd $120 3rd $80
31-40 1st $280 2nd 210 3rd $140 4th $70

Classes:TURBO, NON TURBO, 800, WOMEN

Race updates will be pushed through the TORCS app created by Thomas Sell
Please download the app and allow push notifications
Check website News Story or TORCS app before you haul!

SUNDAY
7:30-2:15 Registration
2:30PM RIDERS MEETING
PARADE LAP
Followed by HOT LAP
then 60 min RACE

2022 FM 109
COLUMBUS, TX 78934
512-632-2369

TORCS TORCSRACING TORCS

CHAPTER 7:
Cole's Fun Pit

On September 8, 2019, Cash and I loaded up Big Blue and drove to Cole's Fun Pit for Round 7 of the 2019 TORCS series. This was our first race after the long summer break, so we were looking forward to hitting the trails again.

WHERE:

Columbus, Texas… it's a small town roughly halfway between Houston and San Antonio. This property has a mix of open pasture areas and tight woods.

Cash and I raced on this property two years ago in what was probably our worst race ever. There were a few things about that event that still haunt me. First, we battled blinding dust that seemed to hang in the air nonstop once the race began. This made seeing and staying on course nearly impossible most of the time. If you stopped long enough to let the dust settle, you risked getting creamed from behind by another racer. If you kept moving forward, you risked nailing a tree or another racer that may be stopped ahead. It was equivalent to racing through the woods with a blindfold on! Very stressful. Second, we didn't finish that race due to a broken ball joint that disabled our old Polaris RZR 900xp. The icing on the cake was getting towed back to our trailer right after the race ended… and in the process, we got soaked by a heavy rainstorm! Mother Nature can be cruel sometimes.

TRACK CONDITIONS:

Just like our last visit here, the track was bone dry and super dusty. At race time, the weather was a toasty 96 degrees and sunny. The only relief from the brutal heat was a nice breeze that blew across the racers while waiting at the starting line. The course included 3.2 miles of twisty trails through thick woods and open pastures, plus a short run through a mostly empty pond.

PARADE LAP & HOT LAP:

When the parade lap started at 2:30pm, 22 side-by-sides gathered near the starting line.

As we made our way around the track for the first time, I noticed the wooded sections did not have any obvious places to pass. Also, there were two places where the track ran alongside a barbed-wire fence, which could easily spell disaster for anyone who gets lost in the dust. Given the fact that barbed-wire fences and I don't always get along (remember the broken wrist!), I made a mental note of those two danger spots before rolling on.

The open areas were much wider and faster and contained several zig-zag turns that made for great power slides. Unlike the rest of the sandy course, the pasture areas were covered with both soft sand and golf ball-sized (or bigger) rocks. In other words, anyone chasing down another racer in the open fields would have to endure both dust and projectiles. Yikes!

CLASSES:

The turnout for this race was pretty good considering the intense heat and dust. There were seven UTVs lined up in the Turbo SxS class. It was nice to see a solid turnout in our class. The next two lines were made up of a dozen side-by-sides in the Non-turbo class, followed by three buggies in the 800cc class (which included one RZR 900xp and two RZR 800s).

STRATEGY:

The biggest obstacle in this race was the visibility challenge that comes from racing in thick dust. The best way to avoid it was to get a good start and hold onto the lead. But that was going to be a tall order for Cash and me.

I don't think I've had any good starts this entire season, and my RZR's slow starting issue seems to have gotten worse every race. I finally decided to do something about it over the summer by upgrading to a new Odyssey battery. The stock battery was 1.5 years old and only registered 80 percent when I put it on the charger this summer. When I installed the new battery a week before this race, I was surprised to find that it didn't solve my problem. After some testing, I decided the fix was a new solenoid starter. So, I ordered one from the local dealership on the Tuesday morning before this race. They offered overnight shipping for $44 extra. Ouchie! But they assured me the part would arrive by Friday if I chose the regular shipping to the dealership. As usual, I took the cheap route and guess what? The part didn't arrive on time. So now we were faced with yet another lousy start for this race and all the dust that comes with it. Lesson learned! Next time, I will spend the 44 bucks for fast shipping.

THE START:

Cash and I were lined up in the middle of the starting line and surrounded on both sides by Can-Am X3s and a few RZR Turbos. Just 20 yards away, the trail made a slight left turn around a stake and then headed downhill towards the first 90-degree right turn pointing into the woods. After a quick prayer and a fist bump with my son, we anxiously awaited the green flag.

The flag went up, and I held my breath as I quickly turned the ignition key. Just as we feared, nothing happened. Dang it! I hit it again. Still nothing. Grrr. Everyone else was pulling away from the starting line in S-L-O-W motion. Noooooo! I jammed the gear shifter into park, then back to High gear, and hit the starter once more. It finally revved to life. What a relief!

As I looked up, I noticed that everyone in my class had disappeared into the dust clouds ahead, except for one UTV on my right that was cautiously entering the dust at a slower pace. I nailed the gas and we caught up to that racer just as we headed down the hill. I somehow squeezed past him on the outside of the first turn and entered the dust-filled woods. Well, at least we were no longer in last place.

In the woods, all I could see was white dust floating in the air. I looked forward, backwards, left, right, up, down. There was nothing but billowing dust everywhere. Where is the trail ahead? Where is the guy behind me that I just passed? It was unnerving to say the least. But my adrenaline was pumping, so I grit my teeth and pressed forward.

LAP 1:

As our Turbo class zig-zagged its way through the first section of woods, I quickly realized that the first barbed-wire fence section was coming up soon on my right side. I didn't want to get caught in that, so I played it cool until we passed it.

The dust was thick and at times we nearly ran completely off course until the air cleared enough to get a visual and make a quick course correction. As we exited the first woods section, we came into a wide section running through a pasture. By now, we were on the tail of another UTV in my class, and I was determined to get around him as quickly as possible. As soon as we hit the pasture, I bolted to the right and slammed my foot into the go pedal. Then I jumped in front of my competitor just before making the next 180-degree left turn. Woo hoo! We just claimed the fifth position.

At the next right-hand turn, I accidentally oversteered as we power slid around it through heavy dust. As soon as I could see again, I realized we were pointed a bit off course and turned back towards the track. Suddenly, the trail turns right again and then runs straight. This short stretch was filled with white clouds of dust and was impossible to see anything. Out of the blue, I hit a small jump (next to a big tree) that I never saw. Oopsie daisy!

A short distance later, Cash and I slid around a sharp left turn and headed towards a large mound of dirt and rocks. As we exited the left side of that hill, we made a hard right and immediately saw Donovan's X3 sitting on its side. Yikes! That scene was a wake-up call to maintain my composure and not get caught up in the adrenaline. The good news was that we were now in fourth position and still on the first lap.

As we continued to race through the zig-zag turns in the open pasture area, we came within 10 yards of Justin McComb's X3, which was throwing plumes of thick dust and tons of rocks out the back. I tried to catch up to him as quickly as possible because we could see the next section of tight woods just ahead. As I flew through the field at breakneck pace, I could barely see the trail ahead in all the roost coming out from Justin's UTV.

Suddenly, my left front wheel dropped into a hole and hit the other side hard. Oh crapola! Was that the end of our race? Did Big Blue just blow out a tire or bend a tie rod? Luckily, my SxS felt normal, and I continued racing. We dodged a bullet on that one because I had just upgraded my shocks over the summer (big thanks to George White at Double E Racing for rebuilding them!), and I'm pretty sure the stock shocks would have bottomed out and been damaged from a hit like that.

Cash and I completed Lap 1 only five seconds behind Justin. We were determined to catch and pass him as soon as we could.

Cash & me after ANOTHER super dusty race.

LAPS 2 through 8:

As the race progressed, Cash and I maintained a five-second gap behind Justin. In other words, we ate a lot of his dust! If we got any closer, the dust made it nearly impossible to see the track and (at times) hard to breath without coughing or gagging. I know some guys use a fresh air helmet system for this situation, but unfortunately that upgrade isn't in the budget for me right now.

Unbeknownst to us, the second place UTV (driven by Chad Helms) pulled out of the race after his fourth lap (I'm not sure why), so that meant we were now in third place. But as far as Cash and I were aware, we were guessing that we held the fourth position.

Somewhere around the fifth lap, we entered the tight, twisty woods just after crossing the dirt road that runs from the property entrance to the parking lot area. One-quarter mile up that trail, we ran through a dusty section where Gil (a TORCS race official) was standing in the middle of two trails and pointing racers from our trail towards the right. Soon after making that turn, the track ran past an old RV parked along the side of the course and then headed to the left where it dumps racers out of the woods and down into a nearly dry pond.

Just as we hit that section, we could see Justin mistakenly went to the right instead of heading straight towards the pond. That's when it hit me! If we were riding on his tail when he made that mistake, we could have passed him.

Soon after that, I caught up to Justin's rear bumper and followed hot on his heels as we zig-zagged our way around the scattered trees in this section of the course. All we needed was for Justin to make one more mistake, and we could finally pass him and get some clean air to race in.

A few moments later, the trail took us back to the wooded area near the place were Gil was directing traffic earlier. This time, he was pointing us to our right to stay on course. But this 90-degree turn was tricky as it included a one-foot trench near the edge of that turn. Just as we made the turn, our left wheels slid into the small trench and immediately caused our RZR to raise up on the two left wheels. Oh snap! Cash and I both thought we were going to roll over. I straightened the wheel and slammed on the brakes. Luckily, Big Blue came back down on all four tires. Cash and I immediately started laughing out loud. What a relief! We fist bumped, and then I hit the gas again.

We continued to hover near Justin's rear bumper for the next lap or two, but couldn't find any safe passing opportunities. Whenever we hit the wide turns in the pasture areas and tried to pass, Justin would roost us with dirt and rocks (a small one tagged my face just below the goggles. Ouchie!)

It was a mad rush to find a way around Justin every time we came to an open clearing, but he seemed to take up the whole track and held us off. I knew we could race faster than him if we could just get around him and start racing in clean air. But alas, Justin played defense well and we never found a clean opening to pass him.

Cash & me celebrating third place.

RACE RESULTS:

When we finally reached the checkered flag, Cash and I took home third place in the Turbo SxS class and fifth overall. Congrats to Kenny Gorman for taking the win in our class and to Justin McComb for finishing second (just a few seconds ahead of us). Unlike the last time we raced here, Cash and I were happy to finish the course. Better yet, we earned a podium finish – which is always nice. I hope we can get a better start next time and give these guys a run for the money.

OCT 5TH & 6TH
STI

Photo credit Tiffany Wilson

SATURDAY
7AM-4:45PM Registration
5:15pm WOMENS PARADE LAP,
Hot Lap then 30 minute race

Gate Fee $10
(under 6 over 60 free)
Camping $10 per night
Saturday Race Fee $50
Sunday Race Fee $90
Membership $45
Transponder $10

GATE HOURS
Friday 5-11pm– gates locked
Sat 6:30am-9pm-gates locked
Sun 7am-3pm

SUNDAY PAYOUT
$50 To Each Sunday Class Winner +
Overall Payout
1-20 1st $120 2nd $80
21-30 1st $200 2nd $120 3rd $80
31-40 1st $280 2nd 210 3rd $140 4th $70

Classes:TURBO, NON TURBO, 800, WOMEN

Race updates will be pushed through the TORCS app created by Thomas Sell
Please download the app and allow push notifications
Check website News Story or TORCS app before you haul!

 TORCS TORCSRACING TORCS

SUNDAY
7:30-2:15 Registration
2:30PM RIDERS MEETING
PARADE LAP
Followed by HOT LAP
then 60 min RACE

738 FM 969
BASTROP, TX 78602
512-632-2369

74

CHAPTER 8:
Rev's

On October 6, 2019, I loaded up Big Blue and drove to Rev's for Round 8 of the 2019 TORCS series. The week leading up to this race was incredibly busy, so I was looking forward to seeing my race buddies again and blowing off some steam on the course.

WHERE:

Bastrop, Texas… it's a small town about 30 miles southeast of Austin. This property has a mix of rolling pastures and woods.

TRACK CONDITIONS:

Last month's race at Cole's Fun Pit was hot and super dusty. Cash and I felt lucky just to finish that race without any damages. With Cole's "dust" pit out of the way, I was looking forward to racing on a track with cleaner air and better visibility. Boy, was I wrong!

Unfortunately, Rev's hadn't seen any rain recently. And it was just as hot (93 degrees) and dusty (perhaps more so) than Cole's. The Rev's course included 3.6 miles of mostly wide, zig-zag turns through open pastures, one small wooded section, and a few dry creek crossings. The main obstacle was finding your way around the track in heavy dust while avoiding trees and other UTVs.

ONGOING STARTING PROBLEM:

This course was very wide and fast, assuming you can actually see where you are going. Getting a good start would be critical on a dusty track like this. And that's what made me so nervous. All season, I have been battling a slow starting problem. Whenever the engine is warm, I usually have to turn the ignition key a few times before it will finally spin the motor and roar to life. This issue has been getting progressively worse as the season continued despite my best efforts to pinpoint the culprit and replace the faulty parts (e.g., battery, solenoid, ignition switch, starter relay, etc.). My latest attempt didn't work, and Big Blue was still not fixed as of race day. Grrrrr.

PARADE LAP & HOT LAP:

When the parade lap started at 2:30pm, 20 side-by-sides gathered together under the hot sun near the starting line. It was time to put your game face on.

Finally, the lead car took off and the racers made their way around the track for the parade lap. Despite trying to keep a safe distance from the car ahead of me, the dust was overwhelming at times, and I occasionally had to come to a complete stop till the dust settled enough to see the trail again. This was especially true in the woods where there was no airflow to disperse the dust clouds that seemed to hang in the air indefinitely.

It was only the first week of October, but it might as well have been Halloween because blazing down that dusty trail while not seeing a thing or knowing where I was going was downright spooky!

Next, the course popped out near the edge of a large pasture and took racers around a huge (dead) tree standing next to a pond. From there, the course proceeded to weave in and around more trees that dotted the pasture. Eventually, the trail winded its way through a small section of trees next to a dry creek crossing. After some off-camber twists and turns through the bone-dry creek bed, the trail directed racers into the open pasture area on the other side of this creek crossing. Here, the soft soil around the large trees looked like silt and resulted in much heavier dust kicked into the air.

At one point, I made a sharp left around a big shade tree and my front wheels plowed through the thick, powdery dirt as I made my way around the turn. Suddenly, the dust and dirt poured up and over Big Blue's passenger door and filled the inside of the cab. The thick dust blew right into my helmet and I had to turn my head to avoid breathing it all in. That dust shower repeated itself each time I hit that corner during the race.

Finally, the trail ran over a straight, but whooped-out section adjacent to the parking lot, then took racers through the scoring chute and starting line area.

CLASSES:

The turnout for this race was normal. There were five UTVs in the Turbo SxS class, 13 in the Non-turbo class, and two in the 800cc class.

NEW STARTING PROCEEDURE:

TORCS normally lines up all racers in the starting area according to their class (Turbo, Non-turbo, and 800cc). Then the flagman starts each class so that everyone in that class leaves the starting line at the same time (except whenever the Non-turbo class is too big to start in one line so they break it into two or more rows with staggered start times per row). But today was different. The track was so dusty that the TORCS officials decided to stagger each racer individually from the start, meaning racers left one at a time at 15-second intervals (similar to the Baja 1000 start). This decision made sense to me given the apparent danger of having five or 10 cars racing around the first few turns in total blindness caused by the extreme dust.

Here's where it gets interesting. TORCS lined up the racers of each class according to their season points. As the current points leader for the Turbo SxS class, I had the honor of starting first. Woo hoo!

My strategy was simple. Get a good start and enjoy the dust-free air for as long as possible.

THE START:

The flagman told me I would be leaving first and asked if I was ready. I was, but my RZR had other ideas. Grrrr.

I hit the starter. Nothing. I tried a few more times while the flagman asked me again if I was ready. I raised my finger as if to say, "just one second." I shifted to park and tried it a few more times. Nothing. Really? Really, really? I'm supposed to leave first, and now my dang RZR won't even start! Now I'm feeling stressed and shoved the gear shifter back into High gear and tried it a few more times. Finally, it turned over and cranked. What a relief! I pulled up next to the flagman and he yelled, "GO!"

Yeeeee haw! I was off and running down the hill towards the first 180-degree right turn. Can you believe it? I won the holeshot!

As a side note, I would like to add that starting one at a time creates a much different feel than starting at the same time as the rest of your class. For one thing, the pressure to go fast and beat everyone to the first turn is simply not there when you leave the starting line alone. Sure, you can constantly remind yourself to go fast and beat everyone else's time, but it's not the same experience as racing shoulder-to-shoulder with other racers who are pushing hard to beat you to the next turn.

LAPS 1 and 2:

After making the first turn, the course ran through a dry, grassy field, then over a small mound of dirt about 18" high, through more twists and turns before eventually reaching a 90-degree, right-hand turn into the woods.

I kept telling myself to remain calm, drive smart, and take advantage of the clean air while it lasted. No mistakes!

Once I reached the woods, I slammed my right foot into the floor and focused on the trail ahead. Going through the woods on Lap 1 with no one ahead of me felt like a dream! It was a straight shot with no dust. I checked the speedo about halfway down the long straightaway and was cruising at 51 mph. Suddenly, the rocky trail turns into soft, sandy loam and continues going straight. I kept the hammer down as I flew through the wooded trails.

Soon, the trail makes a sharp left and goes straight through the woods another few hundred yards with the exception of one small section where the trail goes around a large tree. I could clearly see this tree now, but I knew it would be difficult to spot later in the race if I was following anyone. At the end of this wooded trail, it made a sharp right and headed towards a large pasture.

Just as I reached the pasture and started to build up speed, I noticed my RZR's black plastic hood was flopping around and about to fall off. Noooo! This can't be happening.

Upon further inspection, I saw one of two hood latches had come undone. To fix this, I had to let off the gas, unbuckle my seat harness, reach across to the passenger side, and re-secure the latch, all while driving Big Blue! This was not hard to do, but frustrating because I knew my competitors were only seconds behind me and I couldn't afford to slow down for this nonsense. Grrrr.

Once the latch was secure again, I noticed a new problem… it took two hands to buckle my seat harness. Ugh! I didn't have time for that, so I continued blazing my way around the pasture without being fully buckled in.

Finally, I slowed down enough to put the top plastic clip together and continued onward without being 100 percent secured into my harness. After a few more minutes of bouncing around in my seat, I finally slowed way down and used both hands to buckle the metal clasp on my seat harness. Now I'm back in business!

From then on, I tried to run a mistake-free race and enjoy the clean air while it lasted.

Photo Credit: Mary Parkinson

LAPS 3 through 9:

In the middle of Lap 2, I finally caught up to the 800cc class. Luckily, the first racer I approached (Howard Brown) let me pass as soon as I got behind him. Then I pressed onward through the dusty trails.

Soon afterwards, I caught the other 800cc racer. This time wasn't going to be easy because the racer didn't give me any room to pass. Hmm. I thought perhaps he didn't see me. So I got right on his tail and yelled as loud as I could to let him know I was back there. But he didn't react at all. I ate his dust for a few more turns until I finally got the guts to hammer the gas around the next big turn and blow past him. It wasn't pretty, but I got around him. Now my adrenaline was pumping!

Soon thereafter, I started catching the Non-turbo guys one at a time. But no one would let me pass willingly. I had no choice but to ride their tail (while eating tons of dust in the process) until I could find a safe path around them. Oftentimes that meant running through the tall grass along the edge of the trail while praying that I didn't slam into a hidden log or drop into an unseen hole.

As the race went on, I started seeing a disabled UTV here or there, especially in the pasture areas. Then I reached a corner near the back half of the course where I saw an upside down UTV just past the large tree. A few track officials were already on the scene to cautiously wave me around the downed vehicle until they could safely roll the SxS back onto four wheels. Not long after that, I saw another one sitting on its side next to a sharp corner, and then a second one upside down at a different location. Every time I came upon one of these "upside down turtles," it made me straighten up and get hyper-focused on the course ahead. Just remember, rubber side down!

As I made my way through the scoring chute for the eighth time, the race official yelled, "one more lap." What a relief!

Then I blasted through the starting line area for the final time, made the 180-degree right turn, and headed towards the first pasture area. Feeling good, I hit the 18" mound of dirt hard enough to launch off it. When I landed, I heard the motor instantly rev up and my RZR immediately slowed down. I thought to myself, what is happening? Did my CVT belt just break? Nooooooooo!

No one had passed me yet during the entire race, and I was so close to finishing in front of everyone. Then I looked down and noticed the problem. Luckily, Big Blue just popped out of gear. Whew! I dodged a bullet there. I put it back into High gear, and off I went.

(1st) Mike Kowis, (2nd) Jared Mear,
(3rd) Dwayne Sanders, & (announcer) Cory Williams

RACE RESULTS:

When I finally reached the checkered flag, I took the win for the Turbo SxS class and also finished first overall. Congrats to Jared Mear and Dwayne Sanders for finishing second and third, respectively, in the Turbo SxS class. Of course, the main reason I finished so strong was that I started before everyone and enjoyed two solid laps of clean air. What can I say? Sometimes it is better to be lucky than good.

NOV 9TH & 10TH

Photo credit Tiffany Wilson

SATURDAY
7AM-4:45PM Registration
4:00pm WOMENS PARADE LAP,
Hot Lap then 30 minute race.

Gate Fee $10
(under 6 over 60 free)
Camping $10 per night
Saturday Race Fee $50
Sunday Race Fee $90
Membership $45
Transponder $10

GATE HOURS
Friday 5-11pm– gates locked
Sat 6:30am-9pm-gates locked
Sun 7am-3pm

SUNDAY PAYOUT
$50 To Each Sunday Class Winner +
Overall Payout
1-20 1st $120 2nd $80
21-30 1st $200 2nd $120 3rd $80
31-40 1st $280 2nd 210 3rd $140 4th $70

Classes:TURBO, NON TURBO, 800, WOMEN

Race updates will be pushed through the TORCS app created by Thomas Sell
Please download the app and allow push notifications
Check website News Story or TORCS app before you haul!

SUNDAY
7:30-2:15 Registration
2:30PM RIDERS MEETING
PARADE LAP
Followed by HOT LAP
then 60 min RACE

5118 Highway 90a,
Eagle Lake, TX 77434
From I-10 & TX 71 in Co-
lumbus take TX 71 south
9.8 miles to US 90 ALT
turn L Property will be
on R in about 4.5 miles.

 TORCS TORCSRACING TORCS

CHAPTER 9:
Stick's

On November 10, 2019, Cash and I loaded up Big Blue and drove to Stick's for Round 9 of the 2019 TORCS series. Unlike Round 8, Cash was available to join me for this event. So, I was looking forward to having my good luck charm and fearless co-pilot back in the saddle again.

WHERE:

Eagle Lake, Texas… it's a small town located about 60 miles west of Houston and known as the Goose-Hunting Capital of the World. This property has a mix of prairie land, rolling hills, muddy creek crossings, mesquite trees, and several ponds. This was the first time Cash and I raced at this location, so we were both excited to see what the terrain looked like and how the course was laid out.

TRACK CONDITIONS:

After enduring extreme heat and dust in the last two races, it was a huge relief to hear that Sticks received rain just a few days before this event. At race time, it was sunny, 75 degrees, and no dust. In other words, it was perfect racing conditions. What more could you ask for?

This course included three miles of mostly wide, zig-zag, off-camber, up and down, pedal-to-the-medal fun. Other than tight woods, this track had a little bit of everything. It had muddy creek crossings, long and smooth straightaways (think highway speeds!), a few rough trails that rattled your teeth, one small section that eventually developed deep sandy ruts that high-centered at least a few UTVs (more on this later), steep drop-offs, a few small hills/jumps, and a starting line at the top of a giant hill. In a word, it was a blast!

ONGOING STARTING PROBLEM:

It's no secret that Big Blue has been plagued all season long by starting problems that caused Cash and I to begin most races near the back of the pack. Despite changing every part of the RZR starting system (except the wires), this problem still existed in the final two weeks leading up to this race. In total frustration, I took Big Blue to a local repair shop (3P Offroad) and let them diagnose the problem. After a few days of testing, they were finally able to replicate the issue. They found that if you turn the ignition switch a little too far to the right, it doesn't make contact and won't spin the engine. So, I could either replace the switch or train myself to gently turn the key until it made contact and started the engine.

I was grateful to finally find the solution, but frustrated in the sense that I had already replaced the original switch and it didn't fix this issue. Apparently, the new switch was defective. Moreover, I didn't have sufficient time to buy another ignition switch before this race. Therefore, I had no choice but to train myself to turn the key gently till it cranked over. This sounded simple, but wasn't easy while anxiously sitting on the starting line with adrenaline pumping through my veins.

PARADE LAP & HOT LAP:

When 2:30pm rolled around, 20 side-by-sides gathered near the TORCS trailer for the riders' meeting. Gil made a few announcements and explained that the UTV course would be located at a different part of the property from the motorcycle course. Then he led racers through the parking lot, down a dirt road past a house, and finally up a sloping dirt road to the top of a giant hill. The starting area for our race was on top of this 100-foot-tall hill with incredible views of the surrounding property. You could see for miles up there. How cool is that?

When we took the parade lap, I had three initial thoughts. First, this was going to be a fast-paced race, especially on the long, straight sections around a big pond near the beginning of each lap. Second, we definitely needed tear-offs for the muddy creek crossings. Last, I sure hoped Big Blue started quickly this time!

Once everyone reached the starting area, the lead car began the parade lap at a moderate pace. Cash and I jumped in line about five cars behind the leader, and we made our way down the backside of the giant hill. At the bottom, the course made a hard left and then followed the edge of a large, rectangular-shaped pond. This straight section was wide, smooth, and covered in short, green grass. The only thing slowing down racers here was a chicane located almost halfway down this quarter-mile section. At the end of this straightaway, the trail made a 90-degree left turn and hugged another edge of the same pond. This section was also long, straight, and relatively smooth except for one section that dropped down slightly and then popped back up about 20' later.

At the end of this second straightaway, the course took riders down the left side of an embankment and then back to up to the right where the trail ran across an area of sparse bushes and lots of deep, soft sand. Just past this area, the trail made a hard left and directed racers across a narrow steel bridge. Then the trail ran to the left again and eventually crossed a muddy creek.

On the other side of the creek, the trail turned right for a short distance and then made a hard left turn that took racers over an eight foot drop-off. Next, racers climbed back up and to the right before making a sweeping right-hand turn around a large tree and concrete picnic table. During the parade lap, we followed several cars that accidentally turned in front of this large tree and we all had to circle back around to find the marked trail again. From then on, it was Cash's job to remind me to turn AFTER the large tree (which he did well).

As a side note, Cash and I don't have helmet-to-helmet radios. To communicate with each other during a race, it's mostly just a matter of yelling and pointing. Sometimes we hear each other, and other times we don't. It's not much different than most marriages.

Next, the course takes racers through more muddy creek crossings, a section of tall grass that ends in an off-camber, muddy left turn, and then over jarring bumps. Eventually, the trail zig-zags between sparse areas of mesquite trees and underbrush and then runs up the side of a large embankment at an off-camber angle. Once racers reach the top, it comes back down the same side of the embankment towards a six-foot hill. If racers hit it fast enough, this hill would launch racers into the air.

From there, the trail zig-zagged through a few more wide trails, over a short, off-camber hillside and eventually across another narrow steel bridge. Finally, it led racers to the road going up to the top of the giant hill where the scoring chute and starting line were located.

CLASSES:

The turnout for this race was typical for this season. We had five UTVs in the Turbo SxS class, 13 in the Non-turbo class, and two in the 800cc class.

THE START:

When Cash and I took our position on the starting line, we were lined up with three Can-Am X3s and another RZR Turbo. To my immediate left was an X3 and to my immediate right was Mike Taylor's red RZR Turbo S. There were two more X3s on the other side of Mike.

As a side note, Mike's RZR really stood out because of its bright red color and tall stance (sitting on 30" tires). I remember thinking those are probably not the best tires for XC racing, so maybe he's a newbie (more on his tires later). Of course, I'm always glad to welcome more racers to our TORCS events, and hope that he races with us again someday.

Due to the limited size of the hilltop area, we didn't have much room to the first turn — maybe 15 yards. It was obvious that this first right-hand turn would probably be a cluster-you-know-what, and I didn't want any part of that. In a perfect world, my son and I would take the holeshot and sneak past turn one without incident. But I've had so many lousy starts this season that I wasn't expecting a holeshot today. Heck, I was just hoping Big Blue would actually crank on the first try! Anyway, my plan is always to somehow avoid the mayhem around the first turn if at all possible.

After our pre-race routine (a quick prayer and a fist bump), Cash and I anxiously awaited the start. Soon, the green flag went up, and I gently turned the key. And guess what? It actually started on the first try. Yippee! Almost in disbelief, I hit the gas pedal and off we went.

As the five UTVs converged on the first turn and jockeyed for position, I let off the gas to see where I might fit in without swapping paint. Suddenly, Mike's red RZR came barreling past me on the right side and squeezed into the crowded field of racers immediately ahead. As we made our way around the first turn, I grumbled to Cash, "Looks like we are in last position."

After another turn or two, I saw the red RZR roll over. Then I replied, "but not anymore!"

When I spoke to Mike after the race, he explained that his front tire came off the rim during that rollover, so he was unable to continue racing. Next time, I think he'll have better luck with smaller tires.

LAP 1:

As the racers headed down the backside of the giant hill, I tried to stay close to Jimmie Walker's X3 in front of us and look for an opportunity to pass. After making the hard left at the bottom of the hill, I hit the "go fast" pedal and quickly accelerated. Suddenly, a huge puff of white smoke poured out the back of Jimmie's X3. I thought to myself, "That can't be good." Two seconds later, Jimmie pulled off to the left side of the track and we blew right past him. After the race, I found out that his X3 engine blew up. Yikes! And just like that, Cash and I moved up to third position. Sweet.

Once we maneuvered through the chicane, I hammered the throttle and we reached almost 80 mph before slowing down and making the sharp left turn towards the second straightaway. Here, the trail was relatively smooth except for the little dip that I mentioned above, which threw Cash and me out of our seats for a split second at 70 mph. Yee haw! At the end of that long section, I locked up the brakes, turned left, and headed down the embankment.

As we continued racing through Lap 1, I kept a sharp eye for the fastest lines over the bumpy sections, around the off-camber corners, through the muddy creek crossings, and across other obstacles.

Cash & me celebrating another fun race together.

LAPS 2 through 6:

After completing Lap 1 in third position, Cash and I pressed on with the hope of catching the second position UTV in our class (Nick Collins). Along the way, we started to get more and more comfortable on the track and reached speeds of 82 mph on the longest stretch next to the large pond and 75 mph on the second straightaway. These fast sections were a total rush.

Around Lap 5, we finally caught up to Nick, and stayed on his rear bumper while I waited for a safe opportunity to pass. Soon, it became obvious that it was going to be a challenge to get around him as he tried everything to block us from passing. If we hit a wide section of trail, I'd maneuver to one side and Nick would move closer to keep me from going around him. If we hit a muddy creek crossing, he would slow down in the mud and try to sling mud on us. Luckily, I managed to avoid most of his roost except for one time when I got right behind him just as he spun his rear tires. He instantly coated our helmets (along with the front of Big Blue) with thick muddy goo. At that point, all we could do was laugh. He got us good. I quickly peeled back a tear-off and kept up the pressure.

When we reached the back part of the lap that runs along the side of a large embankment, I came down on the left side and Nick was on the right side. We both raced feverishly towards the six foot hill. Nick hit it first and flew crooked through the air. Cash and I hit the hill at a fast pace, and we sprung into the air just next to Nick. Nick landed to our immediate right, and we both fought hard to reach the next corner first. But alas, he got there a split second sooner and cut us off. That exchange was intense, but I wasn't about to give up.

Soon, we rounded a sharp, right-hand turn onto a very wide section of pasture. We ran to the far left side and I pushed Big Blue as fast as it could accelerate. Nick tried to cut me off again, but I got around him just in time to make the next left turn. Then Cash and I hit the off-camber hillside first and launched into the air. We landed just ahead of Nick and I was thrilled to finally get ahead of him!

Sadly, the sweet taste of victory lasted only a few milli-seconds. Upon landing, I heard Big Blue rev up and felt it slowing down. I knew immediately what happened. My transmission popped out of gear again, which it tends to do when landing big jumps. Dang it! Cash and I worked so hard to finally pass Nick, only to watch him take the lead again while I pulled over to shift it back into High gear. Grrr.

When we started Lap 6, I told Cash this was our lap to pass Nick. No more messing around. We followed Nick closely on the long, straight section next to the large pond, but he moved in front of us whenever we tried to go around him. This was going to be a long, tough race unless we could finally find a way to pass him.

Later, we came to the back half of the course where the large embankment and small hill/jump were located. This time I was patient and didn't try to force anything. A few seconds later, we followed Nick around the sharp right turn that goes into a wide pasture area. As we made this turn, I watched Nick oversteer towards the right and spun out a bit. This was the opportunity I had been waiting for! So, I quickly passed him on the left and never looked back. Now Cash and I were in second position and closing in on first. Woo hoo!

LAPS 7 through 12:

At the beginning of Lap 8, I stayed on the gas a bit longer and hit 83 mph. That was a big thrill! After we exited the second straight section, we made a left turn and ran down the embankment. At this point, I'm getting a bit tired and was only focused on the trail immediately in front of Big Blue. Suddenly, Cash yells at me and points straight ahead. That's when I noticed a few UTVs stuck in the deep sandy ruts just ahead of us. One guy was out of his UTV and pointed towards the right, so I steered in that direction around the bottleneck and kept going. Cash saved the day! If I had kept going, I'm sure I would have ended up stuck in the ruts behind those guys.

As we left the scoring chute to begin the 12th and final lap, I saw my old buddy Dwight Childs and his teenage son, Seth, catching up to us in their orange

Yamaha UTV (Non-turbo class). Dwight is always fast in the tight, twisty trails, but I knew that Big Blue was probably faster on the long straightaways. So, my goal was to see if I could hold them off during the final lap. To do this, my plan was simple. I would try to get as much distance on him as possible during the fast sections around the large pond and then try to hold him off as best as I could the rest of the lap until we reached the checkered flag.

As we turned onto the first long stretch around the large pond, I noticed up ahead that part of the chicane was knocked down. So effectively, there was nothing to slow down racers on this stretch. I kept the hammer down for as long as possible and we hit 84 mph near the end. Yee haw! This was the fastest speed that Cash or I have ever hit during a XC race, and we loved every hair-raising second of it. More importantly, we gained several car lengths on Dwight and Seth.

Next, we raced down the second long straightaway and peaked out at 77 mph. What a rush!

Now it was just a matter of driving smart and holding them off for the rest of the lap, which is exactly what we did. We ended up finishing just in front of them. Of course, Dwight and Seth finished their race in less time than Cash and me, so they clearly beat us. But it was still fun to hold them off during the final lap. It reminded me of the fun times we used to have when we both raced a Polaris 900xp in the Non-turbo class a few years ago. Dwight was always a great competitor. Those were good times!

Cash & me celebrating our first win of the season together.

RACE RESULTS:

When we finally reached the checkered flag, Cash and I were surprised to discover that we took the win in the Turbo SxS class. Donovan Willis was leading for much of the race until he had to stop after Lap 8 for more fuel. Even with that unexpected delay, he was able to take a respectful second place because the other competitors in our class got a DNF (meaning they did not finish). This was such a fun race and a memory that Cash and I will both cherish for many years to come.

GRAPHICSGUYS MOTORSPORTS

RUSTY'S
DEC 7 & 8
STI

SATURDAY
7AM-4:45PM Registration
5pm WOMENS PARADE LAP,
then 30 minute race

Gate Fee $10
(under 6 over 60 free)
Camping $10 per night
Saturday Race Fee $50
Sunday Race Fee $90
Membership $45
Transponder $10

GATE HOURS
Friday 5-11pm-- gates locked
Sat 6:30am-9pm-gates locked
Sun 7am-3pm

SUNDAY PAYOUT
$50 To Each Sunday Class Winner +
Overall Payout
1-20 1st $120 2nd $80
21-30 1st $200 2nd $120 3rd $80
31-40 1st $280 2nd 210 3rd $140 4th $70

Classes: TURBO, NON TURBO, 800, WOMEN

Race updates will be pushed through the TORCS app created by Thomas Sell
Please download the app and allow push notifications
Check website News Story or TORCS app before you haul!

 TORCS TORCSRACING TORCS

SUNDAY
7:30-2:15 Registration
2:30PM RIDERS MEETING
PARADE LAP
Followed by HOT LAP
then 60 min RACE

From Hwy 71 & FM 20 outside
of Bastrop take FM 20 South for
6.2 miles to Pleasant
Chapel Rd, turn R go .02
miles track will be on left.

394 Pleasant Chapel Rd,
Cedar Creek, TX 78612

95

CHAPTER 10:
Rusty's Walnut Creek 2.0

On December 8, 2019, I loaded up Big Blue and drove to Rusty's Walnut Creek for Round 10 of the 2019 TORCS series. This was our last race of the season, so I was hoping to finish strong and retain my season points lead in the Turbo SxS class. Unfortunately, Cash was unavailable to join me this time because he was at home studying for final exams.

WHERE:

Rockne, Texas... it's a small town 30 miles southeast of Austin. At the entrance of the property, there is a large open pasture that served as the parking area and gave access to the wooded trails located in the back part of the property. We raced on this property in late June for Round 6, so I was already familiar with the general layout and terrain.

TRACK CONDITIONS:

Our last race on this property had completely different conditions thanks to recent rains that turned parts of the course into a sloppy mess. In sharp contrast, this race was dry and dusty. While dust was a factor this time, visibility only seemed to be a challenge whenever we followed another racer closely. Otherwise, it wasn't too bad.

Like the last time we raced here, this track was laid out on 3.7 miles of twisty trails through a nice combo of tight woods and open areas.

PARADE LAP & HOT LAP:

When the parade lap started around 2:30pm, 21 side-by-sides gathered near the starting line in a small open area near the scoring chute.

As we made our way around the track for the first time, my initial impression was that it looked similar to the last race on this property, except that it had a few more tight, twisty sections added.

About one mile into the course, the trail made a 90-degree left turn through an open gate. This turn was narrow and a bit tricky, but I made it through on my first attempt and kept going. Soon after that, we reached the low-lying areas with wide trails that ran in between and around large walnut trees. This section was fast and smooth, but some of the thick wooded sections on the course contained rough trails. After the race got underway, many of these bumpy areas eventually smoothed out. As for other bumpy sections, I found alternate lines around them.

Near the end of the lap, the trail took racers through another open gate. The opening was just wide enough for one UTV to pass through easily, so it wasn't a big deal during the slow parade lap. But as the pace usually sped up during the actual race, everything, including this little gate crossing, became more challenging. Each time I flew through this small opening at 40-plus mph, I would grip the steering wheel extra tight, hold my breath, and pray that I would squeeze through without incident. This was definitely not the time to take your eyes off the course and check your phone for messages.

CLASSES:

The turnout for this race was typical for this season. There were four UTVs competing in my class, 15 side-by-sides in the Non-turbo class, plus two buggies representing the 800cc class.

THE START:

A few minutes before the start, the TORCS track officials informed the racers that they re-routed a section of the course so that we entered the first open gate "head on" instead of making a sharp left turn. Apparently, some of the UTVs had trouble during the parade lap and couldn't make this turn without stopping and backing up. This last-minute change was welcome news, but also a bit unnerving as I didn't recall exactly where the gate was located. As long as I paid attention to the track markers, I figured I'd be okay.

The racers lined up on the starting line between two flag poles located near the center of the open field. The first turn was approximately 60' ahead of the Turbo SxS racers on the front row. I took the far left side of the starting line, which left three Can-Am X3s to my right driven by Nick, Jimmie, and Dwayne.

Finally, the flagman raised the green flag and I turned the key. Unlike the last time I raced here, Big Blue cranked up when I first hit the starter. Yippee! As you may recall, I have fought starting problems all season long, but it finally seems to be fixed now thanks to a new ignition key switch.

SIDE NOTE:

While I'm super relieved to finally have that minor issue behind me, I'm now battling a new issue that is a bit more troubling. In past races, my transmission would occasionally pop out of gear whenever I landed from a big jump. This was rare and more of an annoyance than anything. Each time, I could simply stop, run the gear shifter to Park and back to High, and then off I'd go without any more problems. In the last two weeks leading up to this race, Big Blue started jumping out of gear at random times that didn't involve a jump (usually after I let off the throttle). Ugh! Adjusting the gear linkage didn't solve the problem, so it looks like a trip to a repair shop is needed in the off-season. In any case, there was nothing I could do to fix it before this race, so I just showed up, said a prayer at the starting line, and hoped for the best.

With my engine alive, I hammered the gas and pointed Big Blue towards the first left-hand turn. On my right, I could see Jimmie approaching the first turn fast. He was slightly ahead of me when we entered the turn, so I jumped in behind him and we made our way around turn number one. After we roared past that turn, I tried to stay to the left or right side of Jimmie's X3 so as to avoid the thick roost filling the air directly behind him. Dust or no dust, I tried my best to keep the hammer down as long as possible because I knew that Dwayne and Nick were not far behind me.

LAP 1:

As our class zig-zagged our way through the first mile of mostly fast, wide trails, I tried to keep Jimmie within sight. Occasionally, I slowed down whenever the dust became too thick to see the course. Then, I'd immediately speed up again and try to catch him as soon as possible.

About a mile into Lap 1, we snaked back and forth around a few trees and headed straight towards the first open gate. This was the re-routed section, and now it was much faster with the tight turn cut out.

After a few more turns, the course finally reached the edge of the low-lying area with large walnut trees. We zig-zagged around this section at a fast pace and soon the trail made a hard left turn up a small, wooded hill. At the top, the trail soon dropped back down and curved hard towards the right. Next, the trail ran through a section of small trees where the sunlight and shade from the nearby branches danced back and forth across my goggles. It was very distracting and looked like a strobe light effect. This light show, together with dust from Jimmie's roost, made seeing the course a real challenge.

After a few sharp, twisty turns through the woods, the trail eventually took racers around a blind left-hand turn with spectators standing to the right. Then racers turned towards the right to go around a large tree. As we approached the tree, I suddenly saw Jimmie pulled off to the left and stopped in front of a ribbon closing off that section of trail. Apparently, he made a wrong turn around that tree! This was my chance to take the lead. Yee haw!

A few turns later, the trail came to the low-lying area again. Here, I hit speeds of 55-plus mph before slamming on the brakes and making a hard 180-degree left turn that took racers toward an old, barbed-wire fence and then back towards the low-lying area again.

Funny thing about that fence. It wasn't until the third lap of the race before I looked past it and noticed car traffic driving over a two-lane concrete bridge just on the other side. Somehow, I concentrated so much on the race course that I failed to see this public roadway just 20 yards or so past the fence. Doh!

Next, the trail directed racers back and forth through the fast section of large walnut trees in the low-lying area. Afterwards, the trail dumped back into the woods and ran over two short concrete bridges that were concave-shaped (sunk in) and just wide enough for one UTV at a time. If you hit them too fast, the back end of the UTV will pop into the air. I was cautious not to go too fast over the bridges for fear that my transmission might act up again.

Soon afterwards, the trail made several more turns through the woods and eventually came to another concrete bridge over a creek. Here, the bridge suddenly dropped off in the deep water on the right side, so it was best to stick to the left side and play it safe. Afterwards, the trail opened up again to a wide section through large trees and then back into the tight woods again before finally reaching the open gate near the back portion of the course.

From there, the trail soon passed through the scoring chute and started a new lap. At the end of Lap 1, I was still in first position and wasn't sure exactly where the second position UTV was in my class.

Photo Credit: Mary Parkinson

LAPS 2 through 9:

About midway through Lap 2, I ran through a wooded section just past the light show area. Immediately before a right turn, I saw a Yamaha sitting on its right side (driven by Cory Williams). I slowed down and cautiously made my way around. Unfortunately, this was not the only UTV that did this trick during the race (more on this later).

A few laps into the race, I could hear Robert Murkofsky (another fast competitor from the Non-turbo class) blazing down the trails behind me. I knew he was moving at a faster pace, so I planned to get out of his way whenever he finally reached my rear bumper. When he got close, I had just entered a section of tight woods and tried to keep up a fast pace until I could find an opening to move over. Suddenly, I heard my transmission pop out of gear and start making that familiar grinding noise from the transmission. I said to myself, "Oh crap, not now!" That meant I had to stop, shift through the gears, and get going again before Robert accidentally slammed into my rear bumper. Luckily, Robert stopped in time and waited for me to get moving again. A few more turns and I finally found an opening to let him pass.

Somewhere around Lap 6, I ran across another UTV on its side. This time, it was turned on its left side near a sharp right-hand turn around a small tree. Unfortunately, there were more trees to the immediate right side of that small tree, so the only way I could see to get around was to slowly roll between the sideways UTV and the small tree. As my front wheels cleared the opening between the tree and the UTV's wheels, I sped up. Suddenly, I felt a thud as my right rear tire smacked the side of the small tree. My heart sank because I didn't know if I bent anything. All I could do was hold my breath and keep driving. After a few more miles on the course, it became apparently that this incident didn't do any serious damage, and I was able to keep racing. Whew! That was a close call.

Later in the race, I let Ken Asklund and Charles Mueller (more fast guys from the Non-turbo class) pass me whenever they caught up to me. At the moment Charles approached my tail, I recall hearing the dreaded transmission grinding noise. Ugh! Not again. I slowed down and moved over on the trail. Just as I came to a slow roll, I heard the grinding noise stop and it operated normally again. At least I didn't have to do a complete stop to get it going again. This happened once more before the race was over, but I was grateful that Big Blue didn't end up disabled on the side of the trail as a result of the transmission going completely out.

On the last few laps of the race, I started to see Dwayne Sanders not too far behind me whenever we reached the low-lying area. Just knowing he was there kept me on my toes, and I pushed hard to stay ahead.

Around this time, I also started passing slower racers from other classes. Howard Brown from the 800cc class was quick to pull out of the way whenever I caught up to him in the low-lying area. Thanks again, buddy!

Soon afterwards, I caught up to an orange Yamaha driven by Jackson Foster that was much slower than me, but he didn't seem interested in pulling over.

All I could do was ride his rear bumper until I found a safe place to pass. As we exited the low-lying area, one of the large trees had a low-hanging branch that blocked most of the path. Here, racers had to choose between going wide to the left or wide to the right to avoid the large branch. The slow Yamaha went right, so I pushed my right foot to the floor and easily passed Jackson on the left. Howard did the same thing to get around him.

Near the end of that same lap, I came across a group of slower racers from the Non-turbo class and the lead car was apparently the cause of this bottleneck. Luckily, this happened during the last quarter-mile of the final lap, so I patiently settled in behind the group and finished the lap right behind them. It didn't slow me down much, so no harm done.

Thrilled that I finished the season with 3 wins in a row!

RACE RESULTS:

When the checkered flag came out, I took the win in the Turbo SxS class and fourth overall. Congrats to Dwayne Sanders for finishing strong in second place (only 20 seconds behind me) and Jimmie Walker for taking third place (and also for taking the holeshot). It was a fun race, and I was relieved to finish without a mechanical (transmission) breakdown.

After this victory, Cash and I earned enough season points to clinch the 2019 Championship for the Turbo SxS class. Winning this Championship was special to me for two reasons. First and most important, I was lucky enough to race with Cash for at least some of the races. Having the opportunity to race together and share this Championship with him is something I'll never forget. Second, this is the first time I've ever won a championship in my class after 13 seasons of racing cross-country on ATVs and UTVs in various local series. It feels good to finally reach this milestone!

CONCLUSION

On January 19, 2020, TORCS hosted its annual awards banquet at Watterson Hall in Red Rock, Texas. At this festive event, awards were given out to the top three season points leaders in each dirt bike and SxS class. To be eligible for these year-end awards, SxS racers must have competed in six or more TORCS races during the 2019 season.

Cash and I were excited to attend this banquet as the champions of the Turbo SxS class, and we celebrated our victory alongside our fellow TORCS brothers and sisters. Unlike the rest of the race season, no one was under pressure to compete on this day. Instead, everyone simply enjoyed a tasty bar-b-que lunch and camaraderie with our fellow off-road racers. Cash and I especially had fun swapping "war stories" with other UTV and dirt bike racers.

TORCS Banquet: Cash & me receiving our Championship plaque, and Dwayne Sanders receiving his second place overall plaque.

FAVORITE TRACK:

Two topics that were on everyone's mind at the banquet were picking our favorite track of the 2019 season and speculating whether TORCS will change up the classes for the 2020 season. For Cash and me, our favorite property was Stick's. This track had everything we love about racing – superfast straights, muddy creek crossings, lots of zig-zag turns, and starting the race atop of a giant hill where you could see for miles. What a fun course!

CHANGING CLASSES:

For 2020, TORCS added a PRO SxS class to the UTV line-up. This class is strictly optional and no one is required to move up.

The upsides of joining this new class is that racers have a chance to earn bigger cash payouts and will start each race on the front row (definitely an advantage in an extremely dusty or muddy course).

The downsides include higher racing fees and an increased competition level. I'll race with anyone, but I'm not interested in racing for money as that often takes away some the fun for me. As a self-described "weekend warrior," I prefer to compete with others who simply race for the love of the sport and are not out for blood. To each his own, but my racing goals are to have fun and make sure that I'm able to go to work on Monday morning. For that reason, I decided to stick to the Turbo SxS class in 2020 and let the big dogs run together in the PRO SxS class.

CON #1 - POOR ENGINE STARTING:

Big Blue suffered all season from poor starting problems, and I ended up changing every possible component at great expense ($1,000) until 3P Offroad discovered the culprit near the end of the season. This mechanical problem made getting the win much more difficult for many races, especially the extremely dusty or muddy ones where passing opportunities were more challenging.

CON #2 – BAD LUCK STREAK:

After claiming first place in Round 1, I went five straight races without a win. That meant having to finish the season strong to maintain the season points lead for my class.

CON #3 – TRANSMISSION TROUBLES:

The occasional problem with the transmission popping out of gear got progressively worse by the end of this season. To fix the problem, I finally took Big Blue to Turner Cycles in the off-season (mid-December 2019). Over the course of a month, this shop replaced worn gears and a bent shifter fork inside the transmission. The repair bill was not cheap ($1,100), but I was relieved to have Big Blue back on the trails in time for Round 1 of the 2020 TORCS series (see the Bonus Chapter below for more details of how this season started!).

PRO #1 – PERFECT ATTENDANCE:

For some seasons, I'm not able to attend every race. But I committed myself to doing so in 2019. Luckily, I was able to compete in all nine UTV races held during this season, which meant getting 10 bonus points added to my season point total under the TORCS rules. Those bonus points gave Cash and me a little more breathing room to secure the championship.

PRO #2 – FINISHED STRONG:

I started the season strong with a win at Goertz Ranch and finished strong with three straight victories. Having a strong finish to the season made the series that much more exciting for Cash and me.

PRO #3 – WHEEL AND SUSPENSION UPGRADES:

Early in the season, I ditched the stock tires and rims for shorter aftermarket tires and wider offset rims. This upgrade alone improved the handling 100 percent! I only wished I had made this improvement sooner. During the summer break, I sent my stock shocks to George White at Double E Racing to work his magic. For the cherry on top, I also upgraded to a Zbroz adjustable rear sway bar near the end of the season. Together, these wheel and suspension upgrades made a world of difference in the handling characteristics, especially when racing through the tight woods. There's no doubt in my mind that these upgrades contributed heavily to my (three-time) winning streak at the end of the season.

PRO #4 – AVOIDING TREES:

One thing I've often noticed about cross-country racing is the fastest machine does not always win. It's a marathon and not a drag race. All it takes is one driving error that can result in clipping a tree or getting tangled up with another racer, and then your race is over. For me, the key to success on the racecourse has always been to run a clean, consistent race at my own pace, and avoid collisions at all costs. You can't win if you don't finish the race. Luckily for Cash and me, we ran a fairly clean race all season and avoided tussles with trees or other UTVs. I can only hope that future seasons will be this much fun and remain trouble-free.

Our best racing season ever!

Overall, it is easy to see why 2019 was a season that Cash and I will never forget. Not only did we take home the Championship, but we also had a blast competing together regardless if it was a mud race, dust bowl, or perfect racing conditions. As always, I want to say thanks to Gil and Jackie Ramos and the entire TORCS crew for hosting such a fun and memorable series. Cash and I look forward to many more exciting seasons of racing with TORCS.

BONUS CHAPTER:
A Father-Daughter Race

On January 26, 2020, I loaded up Big Blue and drove two and one-half hours to Goertz Ranch for Round 1 of the 2020 TORCS series. I always look forward to racing on this property because the course is fast and wide. A year ago, I was lucky enough to win the TORCS season opener in the Turbo SxS class at this track, so I was hoping for a repeat this year.

WHERE:

Rockne, Texas… it's just a dot on the map about eight clicks south of Bastrop. This picturesque property has mature pecan groves, open pasture areas, and a few creek crossings running here and there.

TRACK CONDITIONS:

When I arrived at the track around 2pm, the weather was absolutely perfect for an off-road race! Sunny skies, 75 degrees, and no dust or mud to deal with. Thankfully, this year's race at Goertz Ranch was relatively dry thanks to light rain that fell the night before which knocked down the dust. A dry race was a huge relief after last year's mudfest on this property where my truck got stuck three times trying to exit the parking lot area. Ugh.

The track was three miles long and laid out similar to last year's course with just a few modifications to keep things interesting. A few spots on the track were soft from the recent light rain, but there was no standing water anywhere.

Unfortunately, Cash was unable to join me for this race because he had a big test to study for. However, I was able to talk my daughter, Lauren, into driving down from college at Texas State University (about 45 minutes away) to watch my race and take pics. I was excited to have my little girl there so she could finally see what her papa does for fun.

When she arrived at the property just 15 minutes before the 3:30pm riders' meeting, I had a little surprise for her. I brought along my old race suit and helmet just in case she wanted to ride with me during the parade lap and hot lap. I told her if she liked these practice laps, then she could decide whether she wanted to join me for the full race or not. No pressure either way. She said yes to the practice laps and quickly changed into her (oversized) gear. Then we hopped into Big Blue and buzzed over to the starting line just in the nick of time.

When we pulled up, we had a good laugh as she discovered the gloves that I brought her were both right-handed! Luckily, she could still wear them, but one glove looked a little awkward to say the least.

PARADE LAP & HOT LAP:

After a short meeting led by Terry Deck and Cory Williams, the racers returned to our cars and buckled up for the parade lap. Lauren and I joined the middle of the pack and all 21 cars began to roll through the course at a slow-to-moderate pace.

My initial impressions of the track were:

- The track was slippery in a few places, especially when circling around the tall trees that are found in the open areas. This means getting traction might be an issue as racers power slide around these trees.

- There were three long and wide straightaways where racers could reach speeds of 60-plus mph and easily pass slower racers, if needed.

- This track doesn't have many technical sections, which makes it ideal for a season opener where you don't want to scare away newbie racers.

As far as my daughter, she seemed to be taking it all in stride for the first mile of the parade lap. Suddenly, she burst out, "Nope! I'm not gonna race with you today because I'm too young to die!" I laughed, and said, "no problem." She is welcome to watch the race and take pics. At that point, I was already proud that she had the courage to do a few practice laps with me, which is more than I can say about my wife.

On Lap 2, Lauren started to feel more comfortable and changed her tune when she said, "if you promise not to roll over, then I'll race with you." Then I was thinking, "uhhh, is she trying to jinx me or what?" Then I assured her that she would be just fine if she raced with me because I haven't rolled my UTV yet. In all fairness, Cash and I have been close a few times though. As you might expect, this exchange left me feeling worried about rolling over for the rest of the day, which is not usually something that I think about while racing. Ugh.

CLASSES:

On the starting lines, there were eight competitors in the new PRO SxS class, five UTVs competing in the Turbo SxS class, and eight racers in the Non-turbo/Open class. I didn't see anyone in the 800cc class at this event.

The Turbo SxS class was made up of four Can-Am X3s, plus Big Blue. In other words, Lauren and I were racing the only Polaris RZR in our class. Knowing that made me feel outgunned at first, but then I told myself that I have the Number 1 plate this year for a reason. I'm just kidding! There are lots of racers faster than me. On this day, the field of competitors in my class include seasoned vets, like Dwayne Sanders, Jimmie Walker, and me. The others were newbies, including Greg Harbour and Oscar Amos. Regardless, all of us were there for the same reason... to kick up some dirt and have fun!

THE START:

The starting line was located between two short flag poles on the edge of the parking area. From there, racers had approximately 50 feet to the first left turn around a tall flagpole. Lauren and I were in the middle of the starting line and surrounded by Canned Hams… errr, I mean Can-Ams.

When the green flag went up, I turned the key and it started right up. Hooray, no more starting problems like last year! I punched the go fast pedal and off we raced towards the first turn. Jimmie Walker won the holeshot (again!), followed closely by Dwayne Sanders and then Lauren and me, as we made our way around the first turn together. From the outside of this turn, I nailed the throttle again and squeezed past Dwayne just before entering the next turn. Yippee! Lauren and I were now in second position and sitting pretty. Well, she was sitting pretty. I was just sitting.

Lauren & me before our first XC race in Jan 2020.

LAP 1:

After we zig-zagged left and right through a few tall trees in this section, we soon came to the first long straightaway. I followed Jimmie down this straight run and quickly hit 60 mph before slamming on the brakes and sliding around the 180-degree turn at the very end. This hairpin left turn has a slick, grassy surface, which made it fun to maneuver. From there, the trail weaves through a few more big trees.

At this point, Lauren and I were right on Jimmie's rear bumper. Suddenly, what I was hoping for happened. Jimmie oversteered as he made a right turn around a slippery corner. He slid off to the outside corner leaving just enough room for Big Blue to squeeze past him on the inside. Woo hoo! Lauren and I are not even halfway through Lap 1, and we already climbed up to the first position. Oh, wait! That means Lauren and I have to somehow hold off four Can-Ams chomping at our heels for the rest of the race. Gulp.

Another few turns later, the course rolls through a dry ditch, which I hit a little too fast and popped up on the back side where my front wheels came down first. I'm a bit gun shy about hitting jumps after having transmission problems last season (but it's fixed now!). So, I decided to go slower through that ditch crossing on the following laps and pray no one gets around me there.

After this ditch, the track makes a left and runs about 100 yards over a nearly straight section along the edge of the parking lot. This was a fast, wide section where spectators in the parking lot could watch the UTVs fly by at 60-plus mph. At the end of this run, the course ran through a chicane to slow down racers and then passed through an open gate. From there, racers entered another field of zig-zag trails that ran between large trees.

After exiting that field, the track goes through a semi-dry (wet sand) creek crossing and immediately made a hard right turn. A few laps later, someone had trouble with this turn and rolled onto their side, which was probably not good for Lauren's confidence.

Not far up the trail, the course made a sharp left turn around a slippery corner and then ran through another big field of big trees. This field contained the longest straight section where I eventually hit 66 mph. At the end of this run, the course dropped down into another semi-dry creek crossing and made a hard left on the other side.

After several more twists and turns through the trees, I suddenly heard my daughter scream loudly in excitement. I burst into laughter because I'm not used to hearing that when my son is in the co-pilot seat. Obviously, Lauren was feeling a bit nervous about flying through the trees at full speed. But I was glad to hear that she was enjoying it so far.

On the back half of the course, racers had to maneuver through a dry, wide creek crossing with a short, steep drop-off and then climb out the other side over a bumpy embankment. When we hit this drop-off for the first lap, I heard another big scream from Lauren. She later told me this section felt like going over a steep hill in a roller coaster. Yep, I'd say that pretty much sums it up nicely.

After several more left and right turns, racers eventually passed through another open gate and made a hard right along a barbed-wire fence. From there, racers climbed through another creek crossing, made a few more turns, and finally reached the scoring chute/starting line area.

Photo Credit: Mary Parkinson

LAPS 2-11:

At the start of Lap 2, I could see Dwayne in my rearview mirror. I tried to put distance on him, but he stuck to me like glue. Whenever I made a little ground on him in the fast, straight sections, he would quickly catch up within the next few turns and start nipping at our heels again. This cat-and-mouse game continued steadily through the first nine laps. Eventually, I noticed that he wasn't in my rearview mirror anymore. What a relief! I later found out he had overheating issues on the last few laps and backed off a bit to avoid engine damage.

On the last lap, I eventually caught and passed some slower racers from the Non-turbo class as well as one guy from the PRO SxS class. That was surprising! I could see Greg just ahead of me as we crossed the finish line. Like Dwayne, he was running strong until overheating issues forced him to back off the throttle. Lucky for me, running ahead of the pack helps avoid this problem.

Photo Credit: Mary Parkinson

RACE RESULTS:

After 11 heart-pumping laps, Lauren and I happily crossed the checkered flag and took the win in the Turbo SxS class. Yee haw! Big congrats to Dwayne Sanders and Greg Harbour for finishing second and third place, respectively, in a hard-fought race. I look forward to battling with these guys and the rest of the Turbo SxS class this season.

Lauren & me posing with our first place plaque.

LET'S GET CONNECTED

I hope you enjoyed this book! If you did, **please do two small favors for me right now.**

First, please take two minutes to leave a short review or rating of this book on Amazon by visiting www.amazon.com/review/create-review?&asin=B0893LBBM9.

Online reviews provide social proof and help me find more readers. Your help in spreading the word about this book is greatly appreciated!

Second, please sign up for my reader's list at www.mikekowis.com/signup/ so that we can get connected. After you join, I'll occasionally share exclusive giveaways and announcements about my upcoming books and speaking engagements.

If you have any questions or wish to contact me about speaking to your group, I'm just an email away! Feel free to contact me anytime at mike.kowis.esq@gmail.com.

Photo Credit: Mary Parkinson

Happy Trails!

ACKNOWLEDGEMENTS

This book would not have been possible without the extraordinary help and support of many folks, including my dear family, friends, and fellow off-road competitors. I would especially like to thank my two fun-loving children, Lauren and Cash, for having the courage to race with me from time to time. Of course, I can't forget to thank my lovely wife (and co-pilot in life) for encouraging me to go racing once a month. Honestly, I'm not sure if she wants me to have fun or just wants to get me out of the house.

Many thanks to Melody Huber for proofreading my manuscript, and also to Kamber Kirchmeier, Jerrell "Rut" Rutherford, Howard Brown, Billy Werner, and James Pierson for beta reading. These talented individuals and die-hard race fans somehow turned my manuscript (also known as a *hot mess*) into something that Cash and I are very proud of.

I would like to give a shout-out to the talented photographers who generously gave me permission to print their photos in this book, including Mary Parkinson (Stop Time Photography), Piotr Mokry (PDMokry), Byron Mowery (GraphicsGuysMotorsports.com), RaceDayPix.com, LapingRacing.com, and Tiffany Wilson.

Of course, I want to give a hearty *thank you* to Gil and Jackie Ramos for granting me permission to re-print their TORCS race flyers in this book and for all of their efforts to host a fun and exciting off-road race series in the Central Texas area. Without their series, this book would not exist!

I also want to offer my sincere appreciation to my long-time friend and movie aficionado, Robert "Ziggy" Parker, for his generous help in refining the "testimonials" for this book. In case you didn't figure it out, I made them up for my readers' amusement. If you didn't enjoy them, I blame Mr. Parker! If you loved them, I want to thank you in advance and let you know that Ziggy played a big part in making these zingers as humorous as possible.

Last, I want to give special thanks to Robert Williams at ILoveMyCover.com for the cover design and to Jason and Marina Anderson at PolgarusStudio.com for the interior print formatting and eBook conversion work.

It takes a skillful and dedicated team to create a book like this, and everyone on my team has my sincere appreciation for their contributions.

ABOUT THE AUTHOR

By day, **Mike Kowis, Esq.**, is a mild-mannered tax attorney at a Fortune 500 company in Texas. By night, he swaps a three-piece suit for a pair of tights and a shiny red cape and then begins his duties as a modern-day SUPERHERO (also known as "Adjunct Faculty Member") for one of the largest community colleges in the Lone Star State. In his spare time, he writes books and competes in off-road races.

In his award-winning debut book, *Engaging College Students: A Fun and Edgy Guide for Professors*, Mike shared the secrets to his success in the college classroom. Specifically, he provided 44 college teaching tips to help any teacher create a fun and lively learning environment, engage students in thought-provoking classroom discussions, motivate them to read the assigned materials, inspire them to attend all classes and stay till the final bell rings, and encourage them to use their critical thinking skills.

In his next award-winning book, *14 Steps to Self-Publishing a Book*, Mike explains in great detail how he turned the manuscript of his first book into a high-quality self-published book. He spells out 14 steps that anyone can take to self-publish a top quality book and sell it on websites like Amazon and BarnesandNoble.com. He also details the costs of his self-publishing journey and shares the top 10 lessons he learned from writing his first book.

In his first co-author project, Mike teamed up with seasoned author and book coach, Sharon C. Jenkins, to write a free eBook, *Maximize Your Book Sales With Data Analysis: The Cure for Authorship Analysis Paralysis*, which is intended to help self-published authors make the most of their book marketing efforts and tackle the dreaded authorship analysis paralysis.

In his next book, *Smart Marketing for Indie Authors: How I Sold my First 1,563 Books and Counting!*, Mike explains his proven book-selling formula and the 16 marketing tools he used to break 1,500 book sales within his first two years of being an independently-published author. He also provides the effectiveness rating for each marketing tactic along with the costs and time commitment involved.

In this book, *Texas Off-road Racing: A Father-Son Journey to a Side-by-Side Championship*, Mike shares exactly what off-road racing feels like from the driver's seat, plus how much money and time is required to compete in this harrowing motorsport. He also shares the gritty details of each side-by-side race that he and his teenage son competed in during their run for the 2019 Championship in a local off-road racing series. Whether you are a long-time off-road racer with ten titles to your name, someone curious to learn about the sport, or a parent looking for exciting father-son activities, this book will surely entertain and enlighten you.

If you have any questions or comments or would like Mike to speak at an event, please email him at mike.kowis.esq@gmail.com, find his author page on Facebook (Mike Kowis, Esq.), or visit his website at www.mikekowis.com.

Made in United States
Orlando, FL
13 October 2023

37851721R00075